BLUEGRASS BLUESMAN

MUSIC IN AMERICAN LIFE
A list of books in the series appears at the end of this book.

BLUEGRASS BLUESMAN

Josh Graves A MEMOIR

Edited by Fred Bartenstein *Foreword by Neil Rosenberg*

UNIVERSITY OF ILLINOIS PRESS *Urbana, Chicago, and Springfield*

Frontispiece: Courtesy of Country Music Hall of Fame® and Museum.

The 1994 interviews are used by permission of Barry Willis and Mike
Dow. Quotes from Bobby G. Wolfe's 1990 serial, "Josh Graves: Father of
Bluegrass Dobro," are used by permission of the author and *Bluegrass
Unlimited* magazine. Quotes from Stacy Phillips's 1993 interview,
originally published in *Complete Dobro Player,* are used by permission
of the author and Mel Bay Publications. A number of the testimonials
in Chapter 9 are used by permission of Betty Wheeler, who originally
compiled them in 2001 for *A Tribute to Josh Graves,* an unpublished
work. Photographs are used by permission of the photographers or their
owners (when photographers are unknown).

Library of Congress Cataloging-in-Publication Data
Graves, Josh.
Bluegrass bluesman : a memoir / Josh Graves; edited by
Fred Bartenstein; foreword by Neil Rosenberg.
pages   cm — (Music in American life)
Includes bibliographical references and index.
ISBN 978-0-252-07864-4 (pbk.)
1. Graves, Josh. 2. Guitarists—United States—Biography.
3. Bluegrass musicians—United States—Biography.
I. Bartenstein, Fred. II. Title.
ML418.G73A3   2012
787.87'1642092—dc23 [B]   2012011210

CONTENTS

Illustrations follow p. 44.

THE DOBRO MASTER

In 1955 Burkett Howard "Uncle Josh" Graves changed the sound of blue-grass music when he added a new instrumental voice, that of the Dobro,[1] to the five instruments—fiddle, guitar, mandolin, bass, and banjo—first heard together in Bill Monroe's Blue Grass Boys of the mid-1940s.

Graves's Dobro became part of bluegrass music when he joined Lester Flatt and Earl Scruggs's band, the Foggy Mountain Boys. Subsequently he participated in all of their Columbia recording sessions except one, more than any other band member.

Lester and Earl hired him to work as bassist and as a comedian in the role of "Uncle Josh." At first he played Dobro only at their recording sessions and on a few pieces in shows. But Uncle Josh's picking was so well received that Lester and Earl quickly moved him to Dobro full time and hired a second comedian, E. P. "Cousin Jake" Tullock, to play bass. Thereafter, Josh and Jake's wonderful comedy routines and singing were part of every Flatt and Scruggs show.

Josh's Dobro became an integral part of the instrumental signature of bluegrass music's most successful band—not just on their chart-topping records but on radio and television and in personal appearances as well. Soon other bands began adding the Dobro to their sound.

Graves not only introduced a new voice to this music, he also devel-oped a multifaceted musical vocabulary for it. He had studied the sounds and techniques introduced by the masters of early country music steel guitar—players like Brother Oswald of Roy Acuff's Smoky Mountain Boys and Cliff Carlisle, who recorded with Jimmie Rodgers. To this he added his own upbeat bluegrass-style picking developed from Earl Scruggs's right-hand banjo technique, which Scruggs personally taught him when they were both working at WVLK near Lexington, Kentucky.

Josh grew up listening to African American musicians in his home community in East Tennessee as well as through radio and records. Still, in those segregated times it was not always easy to meet with, listen to, or play with musicians across color lines. To do this took determination and social grace, and Josh had those qualities. Throughout his life he sang and played the blues, collected blues recordings, and counted famous bluesmen like Lightnin' Hopkins among his personal friends. To me his signal contribution came as he added the rhythms and licks of this music he loved and believed in to the bluegrass sound.

Starting in the mid-1950s, each new Flatt and Scruggs single had Josh's picking front and center. Pieces like "Big Black Train," with its bluesy Dobro opening, drew even teenage fans with a taste for rhythm and blues and the era's new rockabilly sounds into this new music. His blues feeling transformed the Foggy Mountain Boys sound. This can be heard clearly by comparing their 1952 recording of "If I Should Wander Back Tonight" (made before he joined the band) with their 1961 version. There are other examples of this kind of transformation with Josh in the band: compare Flatt and Scruggs's 1950 Columbia recording of "I'm Head Over Heels in Love" with Lester's 1971 version on RCA.

Graves worked with other top acts besides Flatt and Scruggs. Before joining them he'd played with Esco Hankins, Mac Wiseman, and Wilma Lee and Stoney Cooper. After Lester and Earl split up in 1969, Josh was a member in each of their bands. In 1974 he began performing and recording as a featured soloist. He collaborated with many other leading performers, like longtime partner Kenny Baker, the Masters (Eddie and Martha Adcock, Kenny Baker, Jesse McReynolds, and Missy Raines), and Red Taylor, to name but a few.

Josh inspired hundreds of musicians to pick up the steel bar and slide it over the strings of the Dobro. Befriending many of them, he encouraged Dobroists to develop their own music, and sometimes even graciously performed with them on their recordings and at their personal appearances.

Josh Graves died on September 30, 2006, three days after his seventy-ninth birthday. It's good and fitting that the story of this talented and influential musician is being preserved in his own words.

Neil V. Rosenberg
St. John's, Newfoundland, Canada

EDITOR'S INTRODUCTION

This book began in an unexpectedly twenty-first-century way. In late 2008 my grandson Zachary had just set up a Facebook account for me. In one of my first posts, I mentioned that I was looking for some new projects. Barry Willis, author and compiler of *America's Music: Bluegrass* (Pine Valley Music, 1989), who saw the post, knew of my sideline career—as a bluegrass historian, journalist, and broadcaster—pursued in fits and starts since 1965 when I attended the first multiday bluegrass festival at Fincastle, Virginia, at the age of fourteen.

Willis asked if I'd like to take up an endeavor he had begun years ago and never been able to finish. Over eight days in November of 1994, he had conducted extensive interviews with Josh Graves[1] at Graves's home in suburban Nashville. Their intention was to work these materials into an "as told to" Josh Graves autobiography. At the time, Barry Willis was a commercial airplane pilot based in Colorado. Mike Dow, a business associate there, had offered the services of his assistant to transcribe the tapes. The assistant was familiar with neither bluegrass nor the southern dialect and expressions used by Graves, but nevertheless she produced, to the best of her ability, a 113–page, single-spaced transcript.[2]

I agreed to review the material, and Barry Willis shipped from his present home in Hawaii a notebook containing the transcript and a handwritten cover note: "To whom it may concern: I, Josh Graves, hereby give my permission to Barry R. Willis and Mike Dow to write my official biography. Josh Graves 3/25/95." It was clear to me that the material would offer interesting insights into the life of Graves and the history of bluegrass music, so I took on the responsibility of editing and preparing it for publication. Willis and Dow transferred their rights to the project; it had been a labor of love for them and would be the same for me. Willis and Dow searched but were unable to locate either an electronic file of the transcript or the original audiotapes of the interviews.

I made a photocopy of the transcript and marked it with educated guesses as to what the garbled or misunderstood passages meant, using my knowledge of the subject matter and published source materials. I also eliminated the interviewers' questions and comments by others who were present during the taping. My assistant Jessica Bily retyped the extensive document, adding copyediting suggestions as she worked. Meanwhile, I consulted with the then editor of *Bluegrass Unlimited,* Sharon McGraw, who suggested I approach Bobby Wolfe in Davidson, North Carolina, for his counsel.

I had known Bobby Wolfe four decades earlier from bluegrass festivals and fiddle conventions. Wolfe was a Dobro picker then and has since become a well-known builder of resophonic[3] instruments and compiler of articles and a self-published book, *The Resophonic and the Pickers* (1993). Bobby Wolfe signed on to the project and agreed to help me with it as best he could.

My next call was to Pat Ahrens in Columbia, South Carolina. I had met Pat during my teenage years as well and knew her skills as an enthusiast and historian of bluegrass matters (Pat is the author of *The Legacy of Two Legends: Snuffy Jenkins and Pappy Sherrill,* 2007, among several other publications). Pat readily agreed to assist; she would approach contemporaries and associates of Josh Graves for photographs and reminiscences and secure their permission to reproduce that material.

One of Pat's early contacts was Stacy Phillips, a Dobro player and fiddler whom I had known when he was a member of the band Breakfast Special in the 1970s. Stacy had written *Complete Dobro Player* (2002, Mel Bay Publications), which included his own 1993 interview with Josh Graves. Phillips suggested I incorporate material from that interview, gave his permission, and arranged permission from Mel Bay Publications. Bobby Wolfe liked this idea and made available his 1990 interviews with Josh Graves for the same purpose. They were originally published in *Bluegrass Unlimited,* which also granted permission for their reuse.

Pat Ahrens approached Neil Rosenberg, the noted bluegrass historian and author of *Bluegrass: A History* (1985, 2005, University of Illinois Press), who has generously contributed a foreword summarizing Josh Graves's career and significance.

Bobby Wolfe referred me to Betty Wheeler, a Dobro player and attorney from Del Mar, California. She had compiled *A Tribute to Josh Graves,* which the worldwide resonator guitar community presented to Graves at the Society for the Preservation of Bluegrass Music of America Awards Show in Nashville on February 4, 2001. Wheeler had hoped that excerpts from that project could someday be published for broader audiences and quickly agreed to collaborate in what was now turning into a much more extensive undertaking than I had originally envisioned.

Over the first three quarters of 2009, I worked to reorganize Josh Graves's rambling discourses from three separate sources into a readable narrative. I felt like a museum curator restoring the scattered pieces of an old mosaic, identifying similar colors and patterns and adding connective material where it had been lost or was needed to pull the image together. My collaborators—Barry Willis, Bobby Wolfe, Pat Ahrens, Stacy Phillips, Betty Wheeler, and Jessica Bily—liked my early drafts and encouraged me to finish the project. Willis suggested I add footnotes to explain references that would be unfamiliar to readers lacking extensive prior knowledge of bluegrass and country music history. The next phase of the work involved sending chapter drafts to my six collaborators and incorporating their many excellent suggestions.

At the International Bluegrass Music Association's "World of Bluegrass" in September of 2009, Betty Wheeler arranged for my wife Joy and me to visit Evelyn Graves, Josh Graves's widow, in the home where the interviews had been recorded and where the couple had lived during much of the period covered by the autobiography. I presented her with an almost-final draft of the book, asking her to share it with their children and let me know if there was anything in it they wanted to correct or that Josh wouldn't have wanted to see in print. On the five-hour drive from Yellow Springs, Ohio, to Nashville and back, I read the draft out loud to Joy, to make sure it retained the flavor of Josh's storytelling and that the sequence and the sense of the narrative were as clear as we could make them. Joy was a sensitive listener and a good critic, as well as a tireless driver.

The last phase was to edit the supplemental material (introduction, foreword, tributes, and appendixes). Thomas Goldsmith, who was one of the readers for the University of Illinois Press, agreed to supply introductions that added context to each section and perform last-minute tweaking to some of the material. My brother John Bartenstein, former

"Hillbilly at Harvard" host Fritz Mulhauser, and Betty Wheeler—all attorneys—helped with the task of securing permissions and a publishing contract. Tim Davis at the Country Music Hall of Fame provided invaluable assistance with the photographs. Joey O'Donnell coordinated the pulling together of countless loose ends. Librarian and bluegrass scholar Charley Pennell of Raleigh, North Carolina, generously prepared the index.

I owe a debt of gratitude, mainly to Josh Graves for living a fascinating and significant life and for describing it so candidly and colorfully. It is clear from these interviews that he enjoyed telling a good story on himself just as much as he loved playing the Dobro. I believe he would be pleased to know that the story of Josh Graves the son, husband, father, friend, and mentor—as well as Uncle Josh the musician—has been preserved in his own wonderful words.

I am also indebted to the many individuals, named and unnamed, who collaborated and contributed to this book. I am grateful to have been given the unexpected opportunity to work with and preserve these materials and—most of all—to get to know Josh Graves so much better than I had during the years that our bluegrass careers intersected.

Fred Bartenstein
Yellow Springs, Ohio

AUTHOR'S INTRODUCTION

There's a story on me, I guess—where I come from and why. There's nothing fake about me. I just play it the way it comes down; I wouldn't hype nobody. And I think you'd rather have it that way. I'm just an ol' country boy still, at heart, and that old brogue[1]—as you can tell—is still there, and it'll never change.

I'd like to dedicate this book to my grandchildren. I've got twelve of them.[2] I hope it will be something that they can remember me by when I'm gone. Maybe one of them—who knows?—will pick it up and say, "Hey, this is my grandfather here in the Smithsonian or the Library of Congress."

Maybe this book will enlighten them a little bit. They don't have time now to sit down and listen to what I have to say, but someday they can read it and see what their grandfather stood for. That's my main thing, and that's all I care about, really. Or it might help some Dobro picker or some musician coming along. That'd be fine with me, too.

Josh Graves
Nashville, Tennessee
1994

BLUEGRASS BLUESMAN

1

1927–1942,
A Tennessee Childhood

Josh Graves's birthplace of Tellico Plains, in southeastern Tennessee, is close to North Carolina and Georgia and not too far from Alabama or South Carolina, all hotbeds of the driving string-band styles that formed the roots of bluegrass music. Graves came from a rough-and-ready background, one he often cited in later life. In just one example, his father, "built like a rock," moved the family to Maryville in a wagon. That was in the lean years, when looking for edible road kill became a daily practice. Hard times aside, Graves's love of the mountains starts, ends, and remains a constant theme of his autobiography.

The young man gravitated early to the sounds of the blues, sitting at the feet of and learning directly from African American and white musicians in his community despite the segregation practices of the time. Even before Graves started life as a professional musician at fifteen, he was already deeply immersed in the traditional styles he heard and played, not only in family and community settings, but also on radio and on recordings.

Graves sets the stage for his personal and musical evolution in this chapter, which includes his assessment of a passel of country guitarists influenced by the Hawaiian style. One youthful encounter, with the influential Cliff Carlisle, proved a turning point and became a model for his own decades of encouraging younger musicians.

⇒ Early Life

I was born September 27, 1927, in Tellico Plains, in Tennessee. Nothing there but mountains, and that's what I love.

The doctor that brought me into the world was named Dr. Rogers. He could drink more whiskey than you can carry in a truck. I was born at home; there wasn't no such thing as a hospital. All the kids were. A midwife would be there, and then the old doctor would come later and see if everything was all right. I remember when my baby brother was born, in three days my mama was out hanging out her washing. You don't see that now. Tough people, you know . . .

My grandmother Graves was a full-blooded Cherokee. She lived to be 103 years old. Every morning and every night she'd turn that jug up and have her shot of moonshine. She had an old sweet-gum toothbrush and hated me worse than a snake. And I did her. She came from Murphy, North Carolina, across ol' Hanging Dog Mountain from Tellico Plains, Tennessee.

My dad, Troy Graves, worked for Babcock Lumber Company in Tellico. Daddy stood five feet six inches, and he weighed near 175 pounds. Built like a rock. I never sassed him or talked back to him. I wasn't afraid of him, but I knew what he'd do. He moved us in order to work for Alcoa in Maryville. We moved in a wagon. Took three days. I was only two or three years old.

My mother, Sara Elizabeth Thomas, was part Cherokee. Mother played an old pump organ. I had three brothers and two sisters. They were Harlan Richard, Buddy Wayne, Harold Ray, Geneva, and Jewel. Coming up in the '30s with six kids, man, it wasn't much fun. Mama would send us down to the road every morning to see if any game had been run over and killed during the night. Burlap for curtains, kerosene lamps . . . and after that, the Depression hit!

My dad was a hardworking man, and he worked every day and raised us. Dad always farmed, even though he worked a job full-time. We wasn't sharecroppers, but he'd make a crop himself and work the aluminum company. When he had a few hours, he'd work for somebody else—picking strawberries or anything to make a dollar. That dollar was hard to come by all through the '30s when I was coming up. He'd always make sure that we had plenty to eat; that's why he worked so hard. And my mother, she stayed right in there and helped any way she could. They canned vegetables and stuff, and we always had a bunch of hogs and a cow. We lived good—actually better than we would now—because there's so many things that take every dollar that you've got. It wasn't uptown, but about all you could expect in them mountains.

There was a lot of unemployment in those days. But when Franklin Roosevelt came in, he had the WPA[1] jobs, and then he came up with the

CCC[2] camps. And that put a lot of people to work. They built roads and bridges. I remember them telling me, in '29 when the banks went bust, that my uncle had $300 in the bank there at Tellico Plains. He lost it all and never would put no money in a bank again . . . never would fool with a bank. I don't know how much money he had when he died. He had it hid.

Up there it's not exactly farming country. You don't have the space like down here in middle Tennessee or Kentucky. They raised a little burley,[3] and that is hard work. I've done that. You have to watch it year-round, from the time you plant it 'til you cut it and get it ready to go to market. And you're just allotted so much for that burley. There is a difference in the burley and the regular tobacco; they make chewing tobacco and cigars out of the burley—it's more of a black leaf.

We had an old battery radio, and we got to listen to two programs a day. Mama had her soap opera she'd listen to, and then cut it off to save that battery. I can remember charging the battery on an old Maytag washing machine. We would listen to *Lum and Abner* and *Amos and Andy*. When Joe Louis was fighting, on a Saturday night, Daddy would take the radio and set it down on the front porch. People who didn't have a radio would gather there and listen to the fights. Of course, you didn't have to use much battery because Joe didn't fool around—they was knocked out by the time they got in there.

I'll tell you how I got the nickname "Buck." I was just little, living back there on the farm at home. I had this little pinto pony. He'd run loose all summer . . . he was wilder than a guinea. I loved to ride a horse back then. My mother told me, "Now, I don't want you fooling around that horse. He'll hurt you." I said, "No, ma'am. I won't."

It was the fall of the year. I never will forget. I crawled out the window one Sunday morning, and I was going to ride that horse. I woke up thinking about that. And I went down there and got the bridle on him. I was so little I couldn't jump on him, so I pulled him up to a stump. And just as I got on that stump, she hit me with a hickory—a whisk, a limb. And boy, she cut me a good one with that for disobeying her.

There was an old man across the creek, just sitting over there. He hollered, "Buck Jones!" That was an old cowboy character,[4] and I went by that all through that country there, and was never nothing but Buck Graves. And my little grandson, they nicknamed him Buck, too.

My daddy whipped me three times in my life. I won every lick he ever hit me. I stole a watermelon, I got involved with a little ol' girl, and I forget what the other one was. I remember every lick he hit me. And it hurt him worse than it did me. I was the one he protected.

When he died he left me $4,000, which I just turned around and gave to my mama. Back when I was a kid, I thought he didn't like me. My uncle, my mother's brother, heard this for a long time. He said, "I'm going to tell you something. That old man loved you better than anybody in the whole bunch." He said, "He didn't want them hard times for you. He was trying to protect you." And it took me all that time to realize what he was trying to do.

In school they called me Burkett. Years later, we was on this tour of Japan with Flatt and Scruggs, and we went to Okinawa. We were up there in this officers' club. And I'm up there just gigging, and somebody hollered, "Hey, Burkett!" Flatt looked around at me and said, "Somebody knows you." I said, "It's got to be somebody from home." This kid was from my hometown where I was raised, and I knew his father but I'd never met him. He was in the Army over there. When they say "Burkett," you know somebody knows you from somewhere. There ain't but five people that I know with that first name.

The place where I grew up, Maryville, Tennessee, is a little college town. I remember in the old days you'd steer away from a college town to do a show. In that little town, if you was a musician they called you lazy.[5] You was a sissy, you know . . . you wouldn't work. I've done as much hard work as anybody, and now we go in and work a lot of colleges.

Musical Influences

I put what musical ideas I had with what I learned from different people. I'm asked, "Did you do this yourself?" And I say, "No. Uh-uh. I'd be lying if I said I did."

I do a thing on the stage about my Uncle Jim up in East Tennessee. He was an old banjo picker, the old frail banjo . . . I call it "clawhammer." I'd go on the weekends and listen to him. He'd play for me. I'd sit right at his feet and watch every note he hit on the banjo.

My mother's people all lived close by, and I'd go down there on the weekend and they had banjos and fiddles and guitars laying on the bed.

They'd say, "Don't you touch that guitar," afraid I was going to tear it up. I was just a little ol' kid and I wanted the feel of it, you know. And that turned me against them. After I growed up and started in the business, I wouldn't have nothing to do with them. A kid can be dangerous to an instrument . . . I know that. But I love an instrument better than anything in the world. Can you imagine me tearing up an instrument?

I had another uncle, John Thomas, that played Hawaiian-type guitar on a Rickenbacker, and he was fine. He didn't do it for a living, you know. They had a little radio program on Saturdays. He and his sons had a group called the Coconut Grove Boys . . . can you imagine that in East Tennessee? Uncle John helped me a lot, learning solid picking . . . clear notes.

And then I remember one old guy, Buck Roper. He was a black man. We never was sharecroppers, but my daddy worked for other folks. We'd rent a place, and this old man lived on that farm way back in the sticks. He lived across the creek from us, and I'd watch him every evening when he came in, and it'd be almost dark. We'd work in the fields as long as we could, and he'd go in and fix him a little supper and light the coal oil lamp . . . kerosene they call it now.

He'd light that thing and he'd get his banjo and he'd go out and set on the steps. Didn't have no porch, just a little ol' cabin, and he played bottleneck on the banjo. I'd sit there, and it fascinated me, the notes that he would hit, and how he'd curl them around. I was so little, I'd be scared to go home by myself in the dark. I'd hear my mama holler, and I didn't want to leave. I'd just sit there and listen and never say a word. Not long ago, I did a thing for the University of Houston on the blues, which is my first love, and I mentioned Buck Roper in that because he was a big inspiration to me.

Back there in them mountains when I was coming up, they'd have little parties at people's houses. Before I really started what you'd call playing, my dad would throw a party, maybe once a month, and he'd hire these two black guys. One's name was Roosevelt Brown, and the other was Wash something. I sat at their feet and stayed right with them when they was playing. One had an old taterbug mandolin, I called it—big-bodied thing— and one had an old Silvertone Gene Autry guitar, I guess it was, but they could play!

Now, my daddy drank. On the weekends you could look out for ol' Troy Graves because he was going to be there with that jug. He never bothered anybody. Back in those days, you know, the blacks and the whites just didn't mix. But he'd hire these two guys, and they'd play for an hour or so, and the old man would say, "Now, boys, I'll tell you, we're going down to the barn and take us a drink." Mama wouldn't let him bring it in the house. He'd get those guys and they'd have them a jug. He'd say, "I don't care if you drink it, just don't get too much."

Those black people helped me to learn the blues . . . ol' Wash, Buck Roper, and guys like that. You've got to learn from somebody coming up. In East Tennessee, where I was raised, they'd have a bunch of black people, and they'd all join in singing while they was working out there in the fields or on a railroad. Man, it was a rhythm that would take an educated professor to figure out. It was in their soul . . . it had to come out somewhere.

The blues is something you can't hardly explain, really. It's the way you feel. It's either about a death in a family or a broken love affair or something like that. Well, it's the same thing in country, but it just comes out a little different.

I was about nine when I got one of those Stellas. One of those sixty-lesson deals at a dollar each and you keep the guitar. The company moved out of town before the lessons were over, so I had me a guitar. I raised up that nut[6] on there. I couldn't hold it. I've got little hands, and I could never make those notes like everybody else did, so I just took a table knife and put me a clothespin under the nut up there and played with a bar.

I'd meet my daddy in town on payday. He had his little place he always sat and drank beer, and I done his running around for him. Like he owed somebody over here, and he'd send me to pay him, and he'd give me fifty cents. That was a lot of money. I remember strings for my old guitar was forty-five cents a pack. It was Bell brand. So on Saturday, if I wanted a little money to go to the movies or something, I'd steal from myself and put back a dime or a nickel. But I knew I had to have those strings maybe once a month. I'd save for that, and I was lucky enough that I could do that with what little jobs I could pick up on the side and save. But you couldn't buy a Pearse string now for forty-five cents, I don't guess. Forty-five cents for a whole set of strings. Can you imagine?

I met Cliff Carlisle—he played the Dobro on some of Jimmie Rodgers's records. It sounded like an old metal National, but I liked what I was hearing. I remember he and his brother Bill Carlisle worked out of Knoxville, Tennessee, in '38, '39, somewhere in there. I was just a little feller, and they played my little home community. The Carlisle Brothers, Shannon Grayson on banjo, and Cliff's boy Tommy worked this little school there. I think admission was fifteen or twenty cents. It fascinated me so much to watch Cliff—and it's like some kid now, they see Kiss or something and go all to pieces. I really looked up to him when I was a kid.

It never shook me too much, this business, but I seen Cliff Carlisle standing out on a school porch—they took intermission to sell their records and what all, I guess—and he was standing talking to a bunch of guys. He called everybody "John." He seen me standing over there, and he come over and knelt down on one knee. I was just a little ol' kid. I'll never forget it. He said, "John, how you doing?" It scared me so bad I liked to wee-wee in my britches. The first thought that came in my mind, all I could think of, I said, "I've got a guitar like yours." I had the old Stella, you know, no resonator or nothing. He talked to me a long time. Now I've got time to stand and talk to any kid that comes up to me, because I always remember what Cliff did.

In those days I'd rather hear Cliff Carlisle sing than Jimmie Rodgers. They both had that old southern brogue, and he could yodel, too. Cliff played mostly with a flat pick. He could play some pretty stuff, and that's what fascinated me. Now Cliff, he'd get in a bind, he'd clown it up. He could be playing some of the prettiest stuff you've ever heard and all of a sudden just laugh right big and clown it up. I compare him to a pitcher that's been up in the big leagues and is coming back down; he throws junk to get by. Cliff, to me, was a great man, just not that great a musician.

That's his old guitar in there. They gave it to me. "Cliff. . . ." I named that guitar "Cliff." In later years, when I came down here with Flatt and Scruggs, his brother Bill Carlisle was on the Opry. They brought Cliff back to the dressing room, and he remembered me, you know, he'd seen me around. I was going to get him to play, and he was so nervous he couldn't play. He said, "You scare me to death." I said, "Think what you done to me when I was about nine years old."

I run into Bill Carlisle every once in a while, and the other day he wanted to know if I still had my old guitar. I said, "Yeah, I just turned down a new Dodge van for it." He said, "Ol' Cliff would be proud." Bill is eighty-four years old.[7] Cliff's been dead for many years now.

I had a grade-school teacher, Florence Kidd, who played piano. She had a brother, Henry Buchner. He was a fine fiddler, and he taught me a lot.

We would get together with some other boys and play there at the school. After the Stella guitar—I kicked it in, you know—I wanted another one, and my daddy bought me an S. S. Stewart. Boy, I thought I was something. And I put the nut under the neck and played it like a Dobro. Then came a Strad-O-Lin mandolin. Along in there I got a metal-body National. I banged on all of them, but I'd always go back to Dobro picking.

I remember during that time having an electric Supro . . . I was going to try that. They don't make them any more. It was a lap steel with a little bitty amplifier. They was just cheap things. I remember the neck was coming off of it. And my dad took a piece of aluminum and made a brace for the back of it. I'd go with this friend of mine to a camp in the mountains to play. Without knowing anything about it, I plugged it in and the whole thing blew up. I'd plugged into one of those old Delco-Light battery systems![8]

I forget what it cost to have it fixed, but anyway, I sold that guitar for enough money to buy me four little pigs. And I raised those things. And when they got rid of them or killed them, I'd leave home. I couldn't be around. I raised rabbits and I'd sell them. Seventy-five cents a pair . . . had more rabbits than you could ever count. I'd do anything, you know, to try to make a living. And I'm still doing it. But I enjoyed what I was doing. Way back there in them sticks, you'd go crazy if you didn't work or do something.

I saw some other Dobro players back then. Clell Summey was with Roy Acuff; he was known as "Cousin Jody." He was Acuff's first Dobro picker, in the late '30s. I liked some of the stuff that Clell did. It had a feeling to it. He wasn't like the modern-day pickers. He did "Steel Guitar Chimes" better than anybody I ever heard beside Ralph Jones . . . Ralph was out of Boston with Jerry and Sky. There was also a guy named Shorty Sharp who worked with Cowboy Copas.

Then I got to hear Oswald.[9] He is the best at what he does, but I didn't go for that style like I did Cliff's. When Oz hit a lick, it was right there. My daddy and brother drank a lot, and they'd go to beer joints that had speakers on the outside. I wasn't old enough to go in the beer joint. They'd bring me a Coke and a hamburger. I'd sit out in the car, and they would play Oz's "Stuck Up Blues" on the jukebox.[10]

My next influence was Shot Jackson. He was with the Bailes Brothers out of Shreveport on the *Louisiana Hayride*.

Another good Dobro player who has been overlooked is Ray Atkins. He was with Johnnie and Jack on "Poison Love" and stuff like that. He played more like the Oswald style, but he had some different licks.

If I copied anybody other than Cliff Carlisle, it would have been Speedy Krise.[11] He played with Molly O'Day in the early '40s. I was on WROL in Knoxville in 1942,[12] and Molly O'Day was on WNOX's *Mid-Day Merry Go Round*. Speedy played some pretty stuff, and once in a while you'll hear one of Speedy's licks in some of the stuff I do. He knew how to hit the right line in a song; I loved his backup.

I'll tell you another one . . . Bob Wills. I always loved his music and learned a lot from their stuff. I don't do the Western swing, but I picked up the licks that they used, the timing and things. I do a lot of Bob's stuff, like "Maiden's Prayer" and several of his instrumentals—"Faded Love" and stuff like that. I never got to meet Bob, all them years. What was so strange . . . when me and Kenny Baker started working together, that's how come Baker started playing the fiddle; he learned from Bob Wills's stuff. Kenny played the guitar 'til he went in the service and got to listening to Wills's records.

I remember my big entertainment was . . . once in a while, my daddy would have a little extra money, and he'd buy me a record, Jimmie Rodgers or the Carter Family. One day he bought me a Callahan Brothers record. The Callahans, to me, was the first ones that ever did bluegrass music, really.[13] We had one of them old Graphophones,[14] they called it . . . you had to wind it up. And then, I believe it was 1940, Daddy bought an electric job. It had a microphone with it. You could pick that thing up for half a mile around on your radio if you tuned it to a certain place.

These old sisters in our neighborhood knew I had this machine. On Sunday mornings they turned the radio on over there and I'd play hymns for them. And one morning I slipped this record on, not thinking. That "Shake It Down, Shake It." I never will forget that: "Shimmy in the sunshine, shimmy in the rain, shake it on down." Boy, you talk about making some old sisters mad! Daddy broke my record and hid my microphone.

My daddy loved music. He was a good harp[15] player, as good as I've ever heard . . ."Fox Chase," old blues stuff. He didn't want me to play at first, but then we'd have a bunch of people in for a party and he wanted me to play. I said, "Well if I do, it's going to cost you." So we finally got him up to five bucks apiece; that was twenty-five bucks, you know, for five guys. That don't sound like a lot of money now, but it was a lot of money then.

Somebody'd say, "Play 'John Henry,'" and you'd go in and play your heart out, and they'd turn around and start talking again. I'd get so disgusted—and I still do. They ain't hearing what you're singing, and five minutes later somebody says, "Play 'John Henry.'" Then's when I put it in the case and walk off, 'cause they ain't heard a thing you've done. Just a loud noise, that's all they was interested in.

⇒ *Leaving Home*

Back then if you made three bucks a week . . . son, that was a lot of money. And I've done just that, worked on the ice wagon, plumber's helper, brick mason's helper. My folks always wanted me to go to work at the aluminum company when I got old enough. But I couldn't see that. I couldn't stand being penned up for eight hours looking at a clock. I wanted to be a doctor . . . a surgeon. I had enough sense to know that my daddy didn't have enough money to send me, so I figured it would never work. Sometimes I still wonder if I could have done it.

I remember the first year of high school my father bought books for me, and I went for three days. I got into it up there with the teachers. I just walked out. And Daddy was working the two-to-ten shift that week at the aluminum company. I went home.

My mother said, "What are you doing home?" I said, "I quit." "*You quit?*" And I said, "I sure did." And she said, "Lord, your daddy'll kill you." I said, "Well, where's he at?" She said, "He's down at the barn getting down some hay." I said, "I might as well get it over with."

I went down there, and he was up in the hayloft forking his hay down. I said, "I want to talk to you." And he said, "What are you doing home?"

I said, "I just quit school." I knew I might as well hit him with it instead of hem-hawing around. Boy, he had a pitchfork in his hand, and I thought he was going to throw it at me. He come down that ladder. That's the maddest man you ever seen in your life.

He said, "I bought you those books to start you to high school." I said, "Don't worry about that, I just sold them." And I did. Before I left there, I sold them books. I gave him his money back.

He said, "I know what you're going to do. You're going to play that damn guitar!" I said, "If I can, I'm going to." He said, "I don't care where you go or what you do. Don't ever ask me for anything, and I hope you starve to death." There's been a few times I've come close to it. That's the only regret that I have, not getting a good education, or at least a high school education. That was like a college education then, you know.

I just decided that's what I wanted to do, and once I make up my mind, ain't nobody going to change it. Never did. Any young guy coming up that picks, I'll tell him, "Go ahead and get your education. You can pick while you're doing that. If you go to college, you can pick a couple of gigs and they'll pay your way." And a lot of them do that.

I took off when I was about fourteen or fifteen. I just fell in love with that ol' guitar. Daddy didn't want me to play, at first. My mother helped me all she could. I don't see where I could have bettered myself more by doing something other than what I did. I've enjoyed this business, although there's been some hard times.

2 1942–1955, A Musical Apprenticeship

As a music-obsessed teenager in East Tennessee, Josh Graves had to educate himself on how to make a living with his Dobro. He embarked on what turned out to be a lifetime of touring, but, more important, he was learning about interacting with other musicians and entertaining crowds. If making a living meant navigating perilous mountain roads, playing bass or mandolin, or wearing a wig and blacking out his teeth, that's what he did.

Great moments in music were happening just as Graves was starting his career and family. Like a whole generation of young pickers, he was knocked out by the "classic" bluegrass band that Bill Monroe put together with Graves's future bosses Lester Flatt and Earl Scruggs.

Graves worked with several leading acts, including Wilma Lee and Stoney Cooper and Mac Wiseman. With his ears open for the highest-level picking of the day, Graves learned his three-finger right-hand approach directly from Scruggs himself. The syncopated, rapid-fire picking patterns merged with Graves's mastery of old-time country and the blues for a new and exciting sound. Graves's innovations transformed the use of the resonator slide guitar as surely as Scruggs remade the banjo.

⇒ Itinerant Young Professional

The only trouble I ever caused my parents was being on the road and being gone. They knew I smoked cigarettes, but they knew I didn't drink much. We didn't even have a telephone. Now, I could call home and say, "How is everything going?" You couldn't do that then. Never even thought about it. I'd be gone for a week or two weeks, and they didn't know if I was dead or living.

When I started in show business in 1942 down in Knoxville, Tennessee, I was working with the Pierce Brothers. We had a little group that we got together and we'd work square dances or whatever on the weekends. In those days you could hang up a window card[1] or something, and it didn't make no difference who you were, you'd have a crowd anyway.

So we'd go to places like Gatlinburg, Tennessee, which was a big resort. We had a little network radio show, had eighteen stations hooked up, and we thought, "Boy, we're in the money" right then. When I started working there, I was the only full-time musician. They paid me $8 a night. The boys I worked for had good jobs, and they'd say, "Oh, just give that money to ol' Josh." So I'd get mine and theirs, too.

When you're young like that, you think the attention and success are going to last forever, but they don't. I've had it rough many, many times back when I was young. You'd go out and barely have enough gas to get to the date, hoping that you'd make something. I remember one time going to Murphy, North Carolina, from Knoxville. We had this old car, and the brakes went out on it. We was working a percentage date, splitting it five ways. We had barely enough money to get back home and fix those brakes.

Today, I watch a crowd. I'm standing on that stage and I'm looking out all the time. People say, "Why in the world do you do that?" Back in the old days, you'd work those coal camps back up in Kentucky or West Virginia, and there might be a beer bottle come whizzing right by you. They had chicken wire in front of the stage in a lot of those clubs . . . "beer joints" is what I called them. There'd be a big fight start, and you had to have some protection. If you go up through there and you look, you'll find out it's still that way in them coal camps. You take a bunch of them old boys, they get paid maybe every two weeks, and you just happen to be in that place at the time, they're going to have them a ball. First thing you know there'll be a fight break out, and you're right in the middle of it. You're innocent as you can be, but not when them bottles come flying.

I fooled around with the guitar, mandolin, bass. . . . In other words, if I worked in a group and they needed another instrument, I'd have to fill in, more like a utility man. I like to play bass. I can play some jazz bass. A guy came up not too long ago and he said, "Man, I want to tell you, I think you're one of the greatest bass players I've ever heard." And I said, "Uh-uh, I think you've got me mixed up with somebody." And he said, "No, I know who I'm talking to." He'd remembered me all that time. And I didn't do the slap, I just did the "phong-de-phong, phong," you know. And I said, "Well, let me shake your hand. You're about the first one that ever come up and said that."

⇗ Esco Hankins

I just kind of beat around different groups for the first year, but I've always managed to make a living at music, and I'm proud of that fact. As you go along in this business, you meet a lot of people, and the word-of-mouth thing gets around. So Esco Hankins[2] was coming out of the Army in '43. That was my first real big professional job . . . what I called it. I went to work with him on Cas Walker's show[3] in Knoxville. We had three radio programs then, and we worked shows every night. They started me off at $35 a week, which was a gold mine for a kid. I didn't own a car until I was thirty-three, but I'd walk around with a roll in my pocket.

I played Dobro, guitar, mandolin, and some bass. Man, I even used to fiddle some. I got into a fiddle contest in Lexington, Kentucky, around 1949 using a borrowed fiddle. Old-time fiddlers Carl Story and Clayton "Pappy" McMichen were there, and I won it. I told Pappy that I didn't feel right taking the prize as I knew I couldn't beat him. He said, "You won it."

Back in those days, I also knew Steve Ledford and J. E. and Wade Mainer. When I had any dealings with Wade, he was on his own. J. E.—with that red bandana around his neck and overalls—was just a jolly fellow. Wade was more drawed back, you know . . . businesslike. Wade had a big old stretched-out Packard when he came to Knoxville. I was working there with Esco. We was off one night, and he wanted me to go with him. I went and picked a little bit with him. He said, "I'll offer you $35 a week." I said, "I can't hardly do that; I'm making $35 where I'm at." He couldn't offer me any more, but he didn't last long there. That's the last time I ever talked to him. I think he's still living.[4]

Every group back in those days had to have a comedian. Esco Hankins had this guy in the group, Wade Cross—little bitty guy, smaller than me. I was playing mandolin, and they brought him in to play electric steel guitar, trying to get a little modern. They wanted me and him to do comedy. So they dressed him like a woman and me like an old man—we were Aunt Jerosha and Uncle Josh. We'd do part of the show, take intermission, and then we'd dress and come out and he'd be standing there in a veil and a little red hat. I'd black out my teeth and wear specs with no lenses in them. I had a gray wig, wore suspenders. . . . If I had to do it now, I wouldn't need a wig. We'd go out and tear it up. Do that now and they'd probably boo you off the stage.

I got the name "Uncle Josh" from a character back in the old days. In the 1930s, there was a man from the Carolinas that did monologues and called himself "Uncle Josh." I've heard tell that he was rich and in show business as a hobby. He'd tell funny stories. . . . I've got about all he cut. One was "Uncle Josh on a Bicycle."[5] That name just stuck. Later on, Flatt and them knew me as Josh. But Stoney Cooper always called me Buck.

➢ Early Family Life

I got married at a young age. I married Evelyn Hurst—I went to school with her—when I was seventeen and she was fifteen. I don't regret that, you know, not one day. Everybody said, "It won't work." You can make things work if you have to. We've been married almost fifty years—I've decided to keep her. We raised a family. We have three boys and one girl: Josh Jr., Linda, Billy Troy, and Bryan, in that order. She's never complained about me being in show business. Evelyn always likes me any way that I go.

I know when we got married and we had a couple of kids, people would come around and they'd want to give the little kids shoes and things that their kids had outgrown. People wanted to be nice . . . they thought it was charity. I didn't want that. I wouldn't let them take it. If I couldn't buy it for them, they didn't get nothing. But that's a good thing, I guess, to hold in your mind. And them boys did. They'll do you a favor, and if you offer to pay them, you play Indians, buddy. If the Indian does something for you, you'd better let him, because you'll insult him if you try to pay him for it. My kids are part Cherokee, and I'm proud of that.

➢ Bill Monroe, Lester Flatt, and Earl Scruggs

I remember the first night Bill Monroe hit the *Opry* with his new band, late in 1945. When Lester Flatt come in on that guitar and that singing that he did, and here comes Earl Scruggs—nobody had heard anything like that three-finger roll. I was working a tent show, and I'd run out to the truck after we'd get through with the show. The tent crew boys were tearing down the tent, and I'd turn the radio on in that truck. I can tell you the first tune Scruggs played on the *Opry*. It was "My Dixie Home,"[6] and Lester and Bill sung it. I'd never heard nothing like that in my life. I thought, "G—dang, listen to that time!" And Chubby Wise in there with the fiddle. . . .

Earl had just went with them. See, he come to Nashville with "Lost John" Miller, and they wasn't doing nothing, and he was getting ready to go home. Jimmy Shumate was the fiddle player, and he knew Earl from Shelby, North Carolina. And he said, "Why don't you come over and take an audition with Bill, he's needing somebody." So Earl went over to the *Opry*. Of course "Uncle Dave" Macon[7] was there. So when ol' Earl hit that three-finger roll, man, everybody was up looking, and Uncle Dave was so jealous, you know, he thought he was the king of the roost there. He never called Earl anything but "Ernest." He wouldn't call him Earl. Everybody was just making over Earl, and Dave walked up and said, "You played pretty good, Ernest. You don't sing any a'tall, do you? And you ain't a bit funny."

I told Lester about a time that Bill Monroe had Lester and Earl, Cedric Rainwater, and Chubby Wise, and they put this songbook on the market. I told Lester, "I kept hearing Lester Flatt and Sparta,[8] Lester Flatt, Lester Flatt." I said, "I decided to buy that book, and I did. I sent off and got it." And he said, "Well, what did you think when you got it?" I said, "You just bored me so bad, I sent it back to you." But I had to see what he looked like.

⇒ *Out of Music for Two Years*

I kicked around Knoxville there 'til '47, and things got really rough. I guess that part of the country just burned out, and I quit and went to work in construction. I'd work dances on the weekends. Now you take a musician, them hands soft as a woman, and get a pick and shovel and get out there and get to digging footers and stuff . . . boy, that was tough. After about a year of that, I really loved it. Then I got into plumbing with these guys I knew, and times was pretty rough. In that section, Alcoa Aluminum was your big industry—and still is, as far as that goes. They had a big strike, I remember, lasted fifty-two days, and you couldn't buy a day's work.

This was early '49, and I'd left Esco, of course, and he called me one day. I was disgusted because work was that bad, and you couldn't live on square dances two nights a week. He asked me to come back and do a show with him up in Cincinnati and record with him. He talked me into coming back. I'm glad now that I did. I did about eighteen records with him, and then I stayed on there with him 'til early '51.[9]

There was a big snow on the ground, and this guy come in and watched our radio program with Esco Hankins. He said, "Son, if you ever take a notion to change jobs, I know a band that you can get a job with quick." I said, "Well, who?" And he said, "Wilma Lee and Stoney Cooper." We had a rough winter and wasn't doing nothing. I was a little disgusted there, so I wrote Stoney a letter.

≫ Wilma Lee and Stoney Cooper and the Clinch Mountain Clan

I forgot about it, and one day I got a call and it was from Stoney Cooper. He wanted to know if I played Oswald's style[10] or whose. I said, "Well, I never tried to copy Oswald's style." You know, I love Oz and his kind of music, but that just wasn't what I wanted to play, so I said, "The best way for you to find out is just buy me a bus ticket to Wheeling, West Virginia, and you listen. If you like it, fine. If you don't, there ain't no harm done."

So when I was going to take my audition with Stoney Cooper, he bought me a $16 round-trip bus ticket from Lexington to Wheeling. That's what it cost then. I ran into an ol' boy on the bus, and I had my Dobro guitar. He said, "You a musician?" I said, "Yep." We got to Columbus, Ohio, and I said, "Let's go get something to eat." He said, "Could I carry your guitar for you?" I said, "Why, yeah." It was a big ol' thing, you know. I had a belt wrapped around it; it wasn't even strapped down good.

He said, "Tell you the truth, my friend, I'm just so broke. I'm coming from Durham, North Carolina. My mother's real sick in New York State." I said, "Well, that don't make no difference." His name was Thomas, Jim Thomas. It so happened that my grandmother's last name was Thomas. I thought, "Well, might be a little kin there or something." I had the money, so I said, "Let's go eat."

Anyway, we talked and we got to Wheeling. I bought him another meal. He said, "If you ever come around in that New York section"—I can't remember the name of the town now—he said, "I'll be there." I said, "I don't know if I'll get this job or not." He said, "Oh, you'll get it."

So I went, and we did a few tunes. Stoney hired me right on the spot. Wilma Lee had gone somewhere to visit her mother. I said, "What's the money deal we're talking?" He said, "How about $50 a week?" And it startled me. I'd already been making that kind of money. He said later that I could have said $75 or $100 and he would've paid me. Well, I didn't want to leave Esco and those guys in a bind, so I went back and I told them I'd have to leave in two weeks or so.

I worked my notice with those boys in Kentucky, and I had to work a dance my last night. Somebody hired me and paid me a few dollars. And they said, "Well, we're sorry to lose ol' Josh. He's going on to better things in West Virginia, and we're sure going to miss him here." There was a truck driver there. I came down off the stage, and this ol' boy said, "Where you going, kid?" I said, "I'm going to Wheeling, West Virginia." He said, "Wheeling? Well, I'm going there in the morning. How would you like to ride in my truck?" I said, "I don't care how I get there if it's going to save me money riding the bus."

I started off on the Dobro with two fingers: a thumb and one finger with a pick. The best thing that happened to me is when I met Earl Scruggs, when I was with Esco Hankins in 1949.[11] Scruggs hadn't been gone from Bill Monroe too long. He taught me that roll, the same time he was teaching J. D. Crowe, who was just a little ol' boy. I bugged Earl to death. I was in his dressing room every Saturday night; I stayed there with him instead of Esco. That got me into three picks. Scruggs taught me timing and when to play and when not to play.

Anything I've done with the Dobro guitar I owe to Earl Scruggs. I loved the sound of the banjo, but I never could play one. I worked out a roll, but it's backward from a banjo because you don't have that high-pitched string, see, and I lead on the fourth string a lot to get into that roll.

When I went with Stoney, I'd done developed that roll. So anything fast—it didn't make no difference—I was right in there with them. I just crossed what Scruggs taught me with what I had out of the blues thing. I've always played blues, and I still get out of the three-finger roll and hit that blues . . . I don't care how fast it is. Of course if I had to do it all over again—old as I am—I couldn't do it.

My wife is the worst critic I've got, I guess. She knows exactly when I'm doing it right and when I ain't. When I got to Wheeling, I told her, "Listen, tonight I'm going to play something." And I did "Train 45" with that roll so fast . . . encored it three times and it just tickled me to death. The guitar was bigger than I was. I only weighed 120 pounds. When I got home, I was anxious to see what she'd say, and I said, "Did you hear it?" And she said, "Yeah, I did." I said, "Well, what did you think? How did it sound?" She said, "It sounded like you was out of tune." She'd never heard me do that roll, you know.

So I was holding that in reserve until I went with Wilma Lee and them. One day Stoney come in, and he said, "Graves, I'm going to tell you. You're not playing like a Dobro, you're playing like a banjo." I said, "I wish to hell I could." I said, "I can sure change that in two weeks." Stoney said, "Oh, no, that ain't what I meant . . ."

There weren't too many banjo players around at that time: Earl Scruggs . . . Larry Richardson . . . Don Reno. Ralph Stanley, when he started, he was doing a two-finger roll. There wasn't too many good ones, really. Reno's style was so different from Scruggs, and I loved his playing, too. He knew that neck on the banjo.

They'd say, "Who do you think is the greatest banjo picker?" I'd say, "Well, I've got two. One of them's Reno and one of them's Scruggs." Because they played so much different. It was just an altogether different timing. There ain't nobody could get it there like Reno could. He could play anything; it didn't matter. But what I liked about Scruggs, you could hear out there what he was doing. He'd lay that big ol' hand down there, with that big thumb pick. When he laid that down, you knew you could hear something.

When Scruggs come out with "Earl's Breakdown," he didn't have the stops[12] on that thing, just regular tuning keys. And he'd turn them to get that note-changing effect. And every banjo picker you'd see playing that tune would do the same thing. So I decided I wanted to do that on the Dobro. I was working with Stoney, and I'd do anything that Earl did. I had me an old guitar fixed to where I could retune that third string. First night I used that, the tailpiece broke. And it come up and hit me upside my head. I guess that put too much strain on the thing, and I took it by its neck and threw it plum across the dressing room . . . broke the neck out of it. Guy said, "You don't want that guitar?" I said, "Give me twenty bucks for it and pick it up." And he did. Just a little ol' cheap thing. Then I realized I didn't have to turn my keys because I had that bar. But I'd do anything that ol' Scruggs did.

Charlie and Danny Bailey was working Wheeling when I was up there. Earl had just come out with that "Flint Hill Special" then. Charlie said, "Come in here, I want you to hear something." We went in the control room, and he played me that record. He said, "You listen to this." Boy, and ol' Benny Martin on that fiddle. I said, "God Almighty!" Charlie said, "You know, I'd give anything in the world to have a banjo shop." I said, "What are you talking about? Why would you want a banjo shop?" He said, "There'll be more necks come off banjos than you ever seen trying to make that lick that Scruggs did."

When I went with Wilma Lee and Stoney, we toured a lot in the northern states, going up east into Canada.[13] With Esco Hankins, I had been "Josh," but with Wilma Lee and Stoney, it was "Buck." He thought that sounded better. To this day, up in that country, they call me "Buck"—"Buck Graves"—because that's what Stoney called me. They won't have "Uncle Josh."

Stoney Cooper's the man that taught me a lot of things: the way to dress on the stage and how to meet the people. He was a great man in his right. You had to go on that stage and—I don't care if it was 104 degrees outside—you had to wear a coat and a tie.

Guys that work with us now, they'll say, "How do you want me to dress?" I'll say, "Dress any way you want to, just don't wear one of them T-shirts or a ball cap on the stage with me. I'll fire you right then." I guess I got that from Stoney. I don't think they have to be all dressed alike. That went out long ago, but they do need to dress nice. I think a man should dress a little different than what's sitting out there in the audience, somebody that just come in off the street. My wife is so strict on that. She buys me suits, and I say, "What am I going to do with this?" And she says, "I want you to look good on that stage like you always do."

Stoney and Wilma Lee were good entertainers. That's all they ever knew. The only thing he studied was show business; that was their life.

We had a big ol' limousine we rode in. We'd get Stoney busy talking in the car. One day one of his records had come out, and he was talking about it. He was following an old farmer in his truck way up there in Maine somewhere. When the farmer turned off, Stoney just kept talking and following him. I punched the guys so they'd wake up and see what was happening. He followed that farmer right to his house. Stoney said, "Well, Jesus, look where I'm at! Why didn't somebody tell me?" We was just letting him go to see what he'd do.

I remember one time up in St. Mary's, West Virginia, we was driving along and somebody brought up the subject of a new record. At a railroad crossing, Stoney was so engrossed in that song he was talking about that, instead of going over the road, he turned right up onto the railroad tracks. Scared me to death! If there'd been a train coming, we'd a' been fixed.

Two months after I joined Wilma Lee and Stoney Cooper, I was working in New York State, and everything I'd do, somebody'd give me a hand . . . just raised Cain in the back. At the end of the show, I found out it was Jim Thomas—that same ol' boy who I met on the bus when I was going for my audition. He had went back home and started doing good and bought a new car and had all this money. He said, "Take my new car and go where you want to, and here's a roll of money." He pulled it out and said, "Here, take it." I said, "Man, I ain't going nowhere."

We got to be the best of friends. He came and visited me at Wheeling a couple times after that, and a year ago he brought his children to see me in Gettysburg, Pennsylvania. I gave him a couple albums and whatever. He gave me an acre of ground on Star Lake up in New York.

He said, "When you're ready to settle down, I'll give you this." And I thought that was great, you know. The guy was broke, and I had a little money. I couldn't see him going without eating. He'd carried my guitar. I'll never forget him. That's the kind of friends you make, you know, when you get down to earth with people.

I worked for Wilma Lee and Stoney Cooper until 1954. We moved from Wheeling and went to WRVA in Richmond, Virginia, and they kind of wanted to go back to West Virginia. I had done moved once and didn't want to do it again, so I went to work with a little group called Toby Stroud and the Blue Mountain Boys. They was paying me more money than Stoney did, but I knew it wouldn't last.[14]

Then Mac Wiseman needed a man, and he knew I played bass and whatever. So I went with Mac all through '54, based in Richmond. I loved Mac Wiseman's singing and his music, but most of the time he's a loner. He goes out by himself, and I wanted to feel secure. We come in off this big trip with Mac, and we was going to wind up in Nashville. He was coming there to record, and he wasn't going to use me—since then I've done several albums with him. So I turned in my notice.

3

1955–1969,
Part 1, Foggy Mountain Boy

When Josh Graves took a job with Lester Flatt and Earl Scruggs in 1955, he was stepping into a vortex of change in the bluegrass universe. Flatt, the great singer, songwriter, and front man, and Scruggs, revolutionary of the five-string banjo, had sought from the beginning to create a sound distinctive from that of Bill Monroe, in whose Blue Grass Boys they met and created some immortal music. The duo left Monroe separately but soon formed their own band, which came to include such strong performers as singer-guitarist Mac Wiseman, fiddler Benny Martin, and mandolinist-tenor singer Curly Seckler. But as long as they retained the same basic instrumentation as the Blue Grass Boys, it was hard to make the distinction clear. When Josh Graves started playing Dobro in the Foggy Mountain Boys in 1955, it immediately sent the band into a new direction, one that no one could mistake for Monroe's.

This chapter offers Graves's striking account of Scruggs's musical, professional, and personal intensity: "I can still feel them eyes on me if I did it wrong." Graves also presents a side of bluegrass that sometimes gets forgotten: its preservation of old-time comedy routines as part of an all-around family show. Along with bass player and tenor singer E. P. ("Jake") Tullock, he created a duo, "Uncle Josh and Cousin Jake," in which both sang and performed comedy. That offered the leaders an occasional break from carrying the show and the audience yet another entertaining aspect to an evening with the Foggy Mountain Boys.

The team had many strong selling points: banjo-driven music that Graves thought was more powerful than Monroe's, Flatt's peerless skills as master of ceremonies, and a broad-based show that ranged from hymns to comedy to low-down blues. They managed not only to survive, but also to thrive during the rock-and-roll years that drove many other country and bluegrass acts out of business.

➢ Joining Lester Flatt, Earl Scruggs, and the Foggy Mountain Boys

I had met Flatt and Scruggs while I was working with Esco Hankins down in Kentucky. So when we got to Nashville, I got a call from Earl Scruggs. Earl said, "We're needing a man, and I wonder if you'd be interested." I went ahead and worked my notice with Mac Wiseman.

We stopped at the old Tulane Hotel. There was a place there called the Pepper Pot; all the musicians hung out there. Stoney Cooper tried to hire me to come back, and I said, "No, I got another job." I called Earl and nobody knew where I was going or nothing until that big Lincoln pulled up there with Scruggs.

Anyway, I went to work with Lester and Earl and them. I went in to play bass, you know, and that was in May of '55. They told me to bring the ol' Dobro guitar along. They wanted to change their sound, make it a little different, but I didn't know what was going on.

I came in to try out, and after two weeks nobody had said anything, whether they liked it or if they didn't like it. I told the boys in the band, "Well, I guess I'll be going home next week," because they hadn't told me nothing and the two weeks was up.

They called me where I was staying and wanted to meet with me down at the old Clarkston Hotel, down at the coffee shop, and I thought, "Well, this is it." So they come in, and they sat there for ten minutes and said nothing. Finally Flatt asked me which I would rather play, the Dobro or the bass. I said, "Well, that's silly. That's like throwing Br'er Rabbit into the briar patch.[1] I'd rather play the Dobro." He said, "Well, we was hoping you'd say that, because we want to try and get away from Monroe's sound." I said, "Well, I'm willing to try it."

Then, there was no such thing as a Dobro in bluegrass music. A lot of people didn't like it at first, but, especially on the old hymns that Flatt did, that's where it shined. The first record we did with the Dobro took off: "Randy Lynn Rag" and "On My Mind."[2] That broke it right there, and it kind of changed everything all the way around.

In early 1956 we was way down in Alabama working. I woke up on the bus and I heard this sound, and ol' Flatt was looking right over at me. I said, "Who is that?" He said, "I don't know, but let's go find out." And it was us—"On My Mind."[3]

You could never read them and tell if you was pleasing them or not. I would always work for a fellow; I wanted to do a day's work and try to do it right. You couldn't get no comment either way. Finally one day Flatt said, "I believe they like that ol' guitar." So I said, "Fine." And I stayed with them, well, 'til they split up in 1969.

I never gave it a thought how well the Dobro fit in with Flatt and Scruggs until somebody told me, "They created a monster they couldn't kill." I wondered what he was talking about. It took a couple of years for it to sink in that he was saying that without that sound in there, they'd go right back to what it was before. It wasn't a planned thing, and that's what made it so good that it happened.

At first my left hand was true, but this right hand just didn't have it; you can hear on some of the old stuff. I wonder how I did it. You know, most of it was fast, and I never used a capo. Boy, you just had to find the notes, and it was tough. One of the first numbers I cut with them was "Blue Ridge Cabin Home." I wanted to use the roll, so I cut me a block of wood for a capo. When we recorded it, I was afraid Earl wouldn't like it, so I did it single-note. I told him about it later, and he said I should have used the capo.[4]

Earl would really put the pressure on me, and sometimes I knew our rolls would clash, so I'd go another way. He was teaching me then, and I can still feel them eyes on me if I did it wrong. He wouldn't say nothing—just look at me. I had to figure a way to get around that banjo. Listen to the records and you'll know we never played over each other. He'd go one way and I'd go another. I guess that's what made it so clean.

⇒ An Ever-More-Popular Act

They made money all the time that I was with them. When rock came in during the middle '50s, we was packing every house that we played. Other musicians would come up to Lester and say, "Boy, it's gone, ain't it?" And he'd say, "Yeah." He didn't want nobody to know we was doing that good. We was packing every house, maybe two times a night. Of course, we had all that TV exposure. We never suffered a bit when rock hit.

I came in May 1955, and Earl got hurt in a car accident in October.[5] He was out for a year. We had different banjo players fill in, but when he came back he meant business. Then it started getting out of hand, packing every place we played. At one time we were in 110 markets with Martha White and Pet Milk. You'd go into some small weed town, they'd swamp you. They knew who you were. That had its advantages and disadvantages.

We'd have coupons on our shows; we'd give out one for five pounds of flour or five pounds of meal. And I'd give them to families I thought needed it. There's people right to this day that's got those coupons, that kept them for souvenirs. I wonder how much flour and meal I've given away in my time. I'd go out in the audience. Cohen Williams,[6] if he was living today, would tell you that Flatt and Scruggs were responsible for the success of Martha White. It was big.

I remember when they brought Flatt and Scruggs to WSM in Nashville. This was before I came with them. They were working at WSVS, a radio station in Crewe, Virginia, and on the *Old Dominion Barn Dance* in Richmond on Saturday nights. One of Martha White's salesmen happened to hear them in Knoxville, and he told Cohen Williams, "You've got to see one of their shows." They did, and Cohen was sold right then. So they'd tape those shows at WSVS and send them back to run on WSM radio at quarter to six of a morning.

So finally Martha White wanted them to come to Nashville. When I came in, they was only doing the theme for the Martha White segment of the *Grand Ole Opry*. On Friday nights they'd do that from the old studios up there where they had a little auditorium at the station. On Saturday night we'd do a Martha White show there. But when they switched us down to the *Opry,* they'd let us do the theme and one song. And finally Earl got fed up with it. He told Cohen Williams and the whole bunch, "Now, we're not going to go down there and do the theme and do one song. If we can't have our own show, we don't want it. We'll just get out of here."

So one morning we was up there recording those tapes and here comes Cohen Williams. He said, "Now, we're going up on this floor here." That's where the offices was then. "You may see some smoke rolling out of those windows, but I'm going to get the job done." And he did. Bill Monroe and all them, they signed a petition to try to keep us out of there. Cohen told them, "Well, it's either my boys do that show or I drop all the advertisement I've got on WSM." That was $250,000 to $300,000 a year. They ain't going to let that go, you know.

So we started doing 8:00 to 8:30 on Saturday night, and then they switched us to 10:00 to 10:15 or 10:30 to quarter to eleven, I forget which. And son, anywhere you'd go you'd hear "Martha White!" When we was in Japan, they even hollered, "Martha White!" They knew of that from the Carnegie Hall album.[7] I used to have to do that cornbread commercial. I'd have to sing it. And then we started doing the theme. I'd do the theme on the *Opry* and then bring Lester and Earl out.

They was some of the luckiest guys. They hit radio just at the right peak, and then they hit television just right. And it worked out pretty doggone good for them. We had six TV shows a week. Our first stop was Gadsden, Alabama, to buy our groceries. Then Columbus, Georgia; come back to Atlanta; then to Florence, Alabama. Florence to Bluefield, West Virginia; then Huntington; then jump to Jackson, Tennessee, on Friday night; then come back and do the *Opry*.

We did the TV shows live for a year, and then we videoed them, when that video stuff came in.[8] And we'd work a show every night. It liked to kill us. And we'd pull off in some grove or something, some truck stop, and just stay the night. We had our beds and everything on the bus and a stove. I did the cooking. We didn't have no time to go nowhere. On the bus it was like six brothers—they fight, you know, but nobody else better jump in.

When we started videotaping these things, we did some in Huntington, West Virginia, and some in Augusta, Georgia. Then we started doing them all here in Nashville. And then they'd bring in an act from the *Grand Ole Opry* as a guest. But the people would rather see our show. Whatever we brought on there, that was the thing. You still go through them mountains in West Virginia and Kentucky and Virginia, and they remember the old days. Everybody had to be so quiet when that show came on. They'd rush home to watch that show. I've never seen anything like it, and I'll never see it again. Nobody else will.

We went into West Virginia advertising Martha White, and they didn't even have a mill in Huntington at that time. They wanted people to go in the stores and ask for it. And it got so bad the company had to rush and set up a mill there. At that time their only mills were in Lebanon and Nashville, Tennessee. They set up one in Atlanta, one in Huntington, West Virginia, and one in Jackson, Tennessee. Just couldn't take care of it, you know. I'd never seen anything like that in my life. It reminded me of the old Hadacol days when they'd go around in these trains and put on shows.[9]

Three weeks ago, I went back to West Virginia, to the old Huntington area. WSAZ was one of our stations all that time we worked in there. Well, we went back to Milton Opera House—they called it Mountain Air Opera House—and old people was coming up and asking for songs that I did on that TV show, like "Alimony Blues" and stuff like that. WSAZ gave me a plaque on the stage, and that meant more to me than any trophy that I've won yet. You don't shake me too much on a stage, but that broke me right there. And I thought that was so nice, that old people still remembered and came back and did that.

≫ Jake and Josh

I dressed sharper with Wilma Lee and Stoney Cooper than I did with Flatt and Scruggs, because I did comedy . . . me and Jake Tullock. And then in later years, they done away with the slapstick and we'd just go out and do a few little ol' comedy bits and wear sport coats or a suit.

Cousin Jake, you know, me and him had a combination there that was hard to beat. I still miss him. He was one of the greatest minds for comedy I've ever seen. We could take nothing and make something out of it on the stage. His timing was perfect. And he was the same way in real life. He'd walk around and have you in stitches. I took the straight part. Before Jake died, Kenny Baker and I used him eleven days on the road, just took him along with us. Paid him good money and just let him go, and I swear he kept something going all the time. He'd come up with something that was so old it was new again.

We had to have a little comedy bit for every TV show. Son, that keeps you digging, you do that many shows around the country! We never got to do the same thing twice. We had to keep a book with all that stuff in it, what we had done. Maybe in a year you could go back and do some of it again.

We wore little black hats and baggy pants on the stage. Sometimes the show might be two-and-a-half hours long, and Lester and Earl would turn us loose for about twenty minutes and just let us run. They'd go sit down and rest, you know.

We'd do a routine called "The Haunted Hotel." Jake would come in looking for a room, and there was no desk there. You make believe, see. So, anyway, he asks for a room. I say, "Well, I've got one room left. Sign right here"—no pen, nothing—and he looks around like, "What's wrong with him?" But he goes along with me and signs the register. We act like I'm putting us on the elevator and I say, "Be careful of the door." And he steps back and I act like I'm closing the door. I say, "Now, this room's on the third floor." And it's the same place . . . we ain't went nowhere.

I help him out of the elevator and give him his room. I say, "We've got nice feather pillows." Jake just lays down on the floor, see? He'd always have a brick to lay his head on, and he says, "This is a feather pillow? Must have come off of a Plymouth Rock!" I say, "Now anything that you need, you just holler 'Charlie over the river,' and I'll be right here." So he lets me start out of the room and he hollers, "Charlie over the river!" And I'm right back there, saying, "What can I do for you?" He says, "I just wanted to see if you'd come when I called you."

I'd get gone again. He's in there by himself, and he decides to take off his hat, and he lays his hat up on a broom in the corner, and a hand reaches out and gets it. So he hollers for me, and I come running. "Somebody stole my hat." I say, "Oh, don't worry about that. That's room service took it out to be cleaned; it'll be back tomorrow." So then he takes off his coat and hangs it up on the broom.

"Charlie over the river!" It's gone. Do the same routine like that, gone to the cleaners and be back tomorrow. So finally one of the guys would have a sheet over his head, and Jake sees this and he starts to run, and I'm coming in about that time. I say, "What's the matter, what's the matter?" He says, "I ain't waitin' on Charlie over the river." I say, "Where are you going?" He says, "I'm going to the cleaners, I'll be back tomorrow!" You know, it scared him so. . . . Little ol' routines like that.

Nowadays you go out there and do things like that, they'd probably think you're crazy, but you could get away with the slapstick back then. People still like humor; the *Three Stooges* is back on TV in Nashville, you know. We thought you had to have on a little suit and things which made it look better. When you was playing the mountain section or the South, they'd look for the comedy. But you don't see it anymore.

It's a strange thing. With Flatt and Scruggs, we started working the colleges. Earl said, "There are doctors and lawyers and everything sitting out there. You're trying to insult their intelligence." But we'd go right back out and do the same routine and just tear them up, only we didn't have the little hats and the red britches on.

Me and Jake did duets. And when Jake died, I just lost any will to even try to sing, but I have to. We had a pretty good duet. It just stretched out the show, you know. Somebody had to do something. Of course there wasn't no better than Lester, and then the quartet. And we'd do trios; a lot of times me and Jake and Curly Seckler would do a trio.

⇒ A Crack Ensemble

Well, you take the routines and everything I did with Flatt and Scruggs and the songs. I had to remember those kickoffs. Flatt might say, "Let's do 'Joy Bells'"; I've got to be ready for that. I've got to know, even if it's not in the same order. If he walked up to me right now and called a tune, bless his heart, I'd know where to kick it off and what key, because I drilled that into my mind and left it there. A lot of people can't do that.

We didn't have to rehearse much. We could do an album in three-and-a-half hours, easy. I hadn't done "A Hundred Years from Now" with them but two times. That's the first time I used "Cliff."[10] I hadn't done that slide from A down to E before; I was just fooling around with it.

Flatt and Scruggs had more drive than Bill Monroe in those days, just hard-driving. Some of the tunes we did were so fast that nobody else could sing or pick them. That's why I had to learn to get the Dobro in there and get out quick. We'd open with a tune like "Durham's Bull," for instance, so fast I don't see how Paul Warren ever played it. Then we'd come right back, and before Flatt said anything we'd go into "How Would You Like Being Lonesome?" and that thing was so fast you couldn't get the words in, and then he'd talk. Then we'd come right back—maybe do a hymn and pick it right back up again with something fast, where it wouldn't drag, so we could keep the audience.

Curly Seckler . . . to me, there's one of the finest tenor singers that's ever been in bluegrass music. One time he told me, "The mandolin is as dead as poor ol' Hank Williams." And I said, "And by God, you've done more to kill it than anybody I ever knew!" All he played was rhythm, you know. But he'd hold that rhythm on you—and he can't pat his hands in time. Now that's strange. But give him that mandolin in his hands! He was the best friend I had when I came to this town. He'd loan me money, even haul me to get beer. And he wouldn't do that for anybody.

Hylo Brown was with us for a while in the '50s. I was lucky to hear that rascal sing, back when Hylo had "The Prisoner's Song," "Stone Wall," and all that. There was something great about that era.

When the markets got so big we couldn't cover them all, Martha White formed another group,[11] and Hylo headed it up. They paid him a salary plus a percentage. They paid the men and everything. They bought him a new vehicle to carry the band. They had some fine pickers: Jim Smoak on the banjo, Tater Tate on the fiddle, Red Rector on the mandolin, and Joe Phillips on the bass. Where we'd go, we'd pack them in, but he couldn't do that. So finally they just done away with that. He came back with us, worked a little while, and then they let him go.

These auditoriums didn't have good lighting, so Paul Warren straightened up some big ol' cans, put them on boards, and made us footlights. That's what we used for years.

We had an old Stromberg-Carlson PA that you could fold up and put in the car. Everyone used one mic.[12] I think sometimes it's better. You could hear our music in the audience. Earl taught us that way. He said, "Now when it comes your turn to play, you play. Do your backup soft, so you can hear the singer and the harmony." If you're not careful, it can sound like five people talking. You don't know what the hell anyone's doing.

Scruggs said, "Play the melody on the first part of your solo, then I don't give a damn if you cut it all to pieces." So I got to experimenting with stuff like the blues . . . a little jazz. Carl Smith[13] said to me one day, "If they find out what you're playing, they'll fire you." I said, "I've got to find out what I'm playing!" I had a music teacher come up to me one night, and he said, "I know you're playing it right, but you're putting notes in there that ain't supposed to be." I said, "Well, it seemed right to me." He said, "I totally agree, but there ain't no way you can write that." I said, "No, there's not."

I've always loved the blues. You've got to feel that music to play it. What bluegrass I do, I put the blues with it. Somebody said if I played the national anthem, I'd put a blues lick in there. Cutting around on a song is something I learned to do with Flatt and Scruggs. If I do "Roll in My Sweet Baby's Arms," or whatever, the first time I play it through just the way it's supposed to go, and then I'll blues it next time. I put in some blues licks somewhere. Most time when I wind up—at the end of a line—I'll throw in the blues.

Your recovery on the Dobro is the prettiest part of playing . . . trying to get out of a lick, trying not to make a mistake, and you're afraid you're going to. If I get in too big a bind, I'll go to a blues lick to get out of it.

I've always put my arm through the guitar strap. When I went to Wheeling, people would write letters in, they thought I was crippled. It looked strange to the audience. But I found out I could move quicker that way. Strung down below your belt with the strap just around your neck, you can't get in and out from the microphone like you should. You couldn't have done that with Flatt and Scruggs. You'd have gotten killed.

I hit Earl one time when I first came to Nashville. There used to be a nice little auditorium over at the old WSM where we played *Breakfast at the Opry*. Earl was doing "Flint Hill Special." I was right behind him, and when he came out, I went in. When I backed out, I went the wrong way and knocked his bridge down. Pow! The only thing I could think of was to finish the tune out. After it was over, I went to Earl and said, "Earl, I want to apologize to you." He said, "You'll know the next time, won't you?"

Scruggs was the best teacher that's ever been or ever will be. He was like a football coach. They said we looked like the Notre Dame football team. Scruggs was the quarterback, and I was the running back. I knew exactly where to go because he told me where to go. He'd hand the ball off to me, and I'd go through that hole. If you didn't get out of there, you'd get stepped on.

The way we worked a stage was pretty to look at from the audience.[14] I remember at Carnegie Hall, we turned it on a little bit more that night. You could hear the audience react.

When I came with them boys, they'd stand there like a statue. I said, "We've got to move this." Even got Jake Tullock into that. He'd come in with that bass fiddle to sing a part and move right back out. I guess partly my doings done that. I don't know, but I knew I had to have a hole to get in there, and I wanted them out of there. I weighed 120 pounds, you know.

Them guys, all of them weighed 200. They'd tromp on you. When a new man would come in, he'd almost get killed before he learned.

Our tuning and timing had to be right, and Earl wouldn't let us pat our feet. He just figured you didn't have to do it to play. Poor Paul Warren,[15] he couldn't play without patting his foot. I've seen Earl walk over and put his foot on Paul's. Paul would start patting the other. Earl just finally gave up. If you listen to the Carnegie Hall album, you'll hear Paul's left foot patting. Earl taught me the rhythm lick, and if you watch me, I'll walk that stage just like he does. Time could be out a little bit, and he'd walk and bring it back together.

Earl didn't allow nobody to tune on the stage. If your instrument was out or you broke a string, you'd go behind the stage, fix it, and then come back. You'd tune to what you heard; you'd hear the beat that was going, join in, and then you walked back out. Earl said, "If you come back out there and your guitar or your whatever is out of tune, you're going to make everybody else sound bad."

There's many nights I've sat right here at this table and worked on perfection. I'd come in, maybe twelve at night, after a local show. I'd sit here 'til four or five in the morning and work out the mistakes that I had done and I knew I did. I didn't have to have it played back to me. I'd go back in the next time and try that lick again, and I'd look at Scruggs and say, "How was that?" "That's all right." He wouldn't say it like I was a little dog that needs to be patted on the head, but he knew what I was doing. I don't do that no more; I don't have to now, thank the Lord.

You had so many tunes, the standard thing, and do them the same way around for maybe a year, and you'd get so sick of that you'd want to scream. Me and Kenny Baker was talking about that the other day, how you could figure every tune they are going to play. When you work with a band a long time, you get where you think, "Well, I can do that with my eyes shut. There ain't no use to rehearse that." And that's bad. Next time you go back somewhere, you've got to change your show. You have to do something else. We'd ride 900 miles and then come in here and rehearse "Roll in My Sweet Baby's Arms." Earl wanted it that way. We'd go back to the basics on our parts.

I learned three-finger guitar about the same time as I learned to put Earl Scruggs's roll on the Dobro. I figured I'd get him on one or the other! I played finger-style guitar with Flatt and Scruggs just maybe when Earl was sick. You know Earl was the greatest on that, too. I'd just as soon hear him play guitar as banjo. I've got to tell you, Earl was the cleanest picker, and he just had the sound. No matter where or what I'm picking, I'm still listening for something that isn't there anymore.

4

1955–1969, Part 2, Life on the Road and the Breakup

Traveling thousands of miles on the preinterstate highways of the South was full of danger and exhaustion for travelers in the 1950s. But just as the Beatles did in their prestardom days, Flatt and Scruggs and the Foggy Mountain Boys honed a hard-driving sound to perfection by near-constant touring. In a smoke-and joke-filled tour bus that often served as overnight accommodation, they built personal camaraderie that was reflected in the seamless rapport of their playing and singing. By those years, the band's lineup was mostly set, with Lester Flatt and Earl Scruggs joined by Dobro man Josh Graves, Curly Seckler on mandolin and tenor vocals, bassist Jake Tullock, and fiddler Paul Warren.

As Graves's account of a dramatic wreck shows, Earl's wife, Louise, and their son Randy (born in 1952) were sometimes along on the bus. Graves offers an up-close view of how the rough-and-tumble road trips turned into college tours, big-city auditoriums, and television spots, courtesy of the folk revival, the Beverly Hillbillies, *and the Scruggs's show-business savvy. It was Earl, Graves reveals, who taught Louise the management skills that made her a role model in her own right.*

Once a music designed, as their former boss Bill Monroe said, for farm and country people, bluegrass rocketed to national and international success largely through the broad exposure afforded Flatt and Scruggs. As the ultimate insider, Graves reveals both the complementary talents and the musical and personal issues that led to the breakup of bluegrass music's most famous duo. For years Lester and Earl were linked in people's minds as closely as ham and eggs, but there were personal and musical differences that grew sharper as times and fashions changed. Graves was able to see both sides of the famous disagreements between the partners, was there for the breakup, and later went on to work with both men in their solo careers.

♦ At Home on the Bus

You don't ride with somebody that long and not think a hell of a lot of them. We had some good times. I've seen us play poker on that bus. . . . I remember one time the generator was going out, and we couldn't use the light back there. We tied a flashlight up over a bunk and played poker. We'd do that all the time.

One time we was traveling when Paul Warren and I first went with them. We was going down through Georgia, and Paul was driving, and there was three in the front and three in the back. They wore them rolled-brim hats then, you know, Stetsons, and we'd take one of them hats and make a pot for the money. Everybody was smoking a cigar—them Red Dot cigars, I never will forget. We was going down through Georgia, through that backcountry down there, and all of sudden, I never heard such a racket. Somebody run Paul off the road. It so happened there was a little road there, and he run through this farmer's yard, into chicken coops. Chickens going everywhere and hay a'flying. Somebody said, "Who's driving?" They said, "It's Paul." Somebody said, "Deal the cards." They didn't care, you know.

Another time, I remember Earl had just come back with us after being off about a year. He had those broken hips. We watched him like a hawk so he wouldn't fall. Everybody was sleeping. Curly Seckler was driving, and the bus caught on fire. I looked out the mirror, and the smoke was just a'rolling. I said, "Seck, see if you can get everybody up, and I'll get the instruments (they were in the engine compartment). I had guitars and banjos strewn up and down that road. Earl was asleep, and Lester didn't want to excite him. He shook him and said, "Earl . . . Earl . . . Wake up . . . Now don't be in no hurry, BUT THIS GODDAMN BUS IS ON FIRE!"

We had two wrecks, but never did hurt none of us. We was lucky. Them old roads and an old four-banger diesel bus . . . wasn't no interstate then, you know. We had one bad wreck over on U.S. 64 in, I believe it was '58. I know it was on my wedding anniversary, the 18th of August, and I had to leave that morning. We was going to Franklin, North Carolina. That was the most miserable week I think I've ever spent in show business. We wound up in Shelby, North Carolina, Earl's hometown. It drove the windshield of that bus back to where you couldn't get your hands between it and the steering wheel, knocked the lights out, and we went on and played in Franklin that night. It rained. God, it rained! We had to stay in Shelby for a week and work out of that town because the insurance people was coming in, you know.

None of us got hurt, but it hurt the people in the car real bad. It wasn't our fault. We was going up that old Highway 64, when I seen this thing coming; I couldn't tell what it was. This car was going around and around. He got on that blacktop, in that rain. The guy was from Memphis. Randy Scruggs, he was just a little feller, and I was holding him up there and showing him bears and everything—to keep him pacified—and that thing come out of that ditch, and I kept thinking, "Well maybe it's going to miss us." Earl pulled over just as far as he could, but he hit us head on. Earl screamed, and I thought, "Oh, God, here he goes again." It hadn't been too long since Earl had his first wreck, the bad wreck that crippled him up. I thought when that car hit that it messed up his legs again.

When it finally got stopped, I couldn't get the door open. Everybody but me and Randy and Louise and Earl was laying down in their bunks. So I finally got out, and there was that car tore all to pieces, and this guy was begging me to help his wife and his kid. But I knew I'd better get on up there and stop the rest of that traffic that'd come right in on him. I was out there in a T-shirt—had my shirt off waving the traffic down. They thought I was drunk, you know. And I heard some woman say, "Them ol' hillbillies just run over them people in that car." If I could have got hold of her, I'd have killed her.

So here come the police, and Lester and Earl was just in shock. They was going to move the car away, and I said, "Whoa, wait a minute. Let's make this report out here so they'll know what happened." And that cop said, "There's no need to make a report. They just run over you people." But we was awful lucky.

⤳ *The Financial Side*

I enjoyed every minute of it. They were two of the most honest guys you'd ever want to work with. They was just as country as could be, but they meant business. Maybe they didn't pay as much as they should have, but they paid you what they said they would. I never missed a payday in all the years I was with them. I didn't make a lot of money until I broke out on my own. Maybe I didn't make as much money, but it was solid. And I was never one to jump out on one of these wild gigs.

When I was with Flatt and Scruggs, I had some of the big guys, even from here in Nashville, offer me a job. I wouldn't take it—and it wouldn't have lasted two weeks where some of them guys was going. Maybe I'm sitting somewhere doing a pretty good gig and somebody comes up and offers me more money. I'd say, "No, I have family coming up, and I want a little security for them. I'll just stay where I'm at." I raised five kids, and I wanted something for them. Didn't matter about me; I can sleep in the car or anything. Every dime that I made, I didn't throw it away. I brought it right here to Evelyn, and she made do with what I had.

Flatt and Scruggs would just tell you what they'd pay, and that was it. You could take it or leave it. But what I could never understand was they'd bring somebody in new and start them off at the same money that you was making. That ain't right when you've been there since whiskey. I never did approve of that, and I told them I didn't. I'd quit and get a raise when I'd come back. I wouldn't dicker with them. I'd just say, "Well, I can't make it on what I'm getting."

The other boys, they'd bitch and go on, but they wouldn't go tell them theirselves. But I'd stand up to them. I wasn't afraid of them. I didn't have to be, and I knew that. But if I work for you for fourteen years without a flaw anywhere, you know when I need a raise and when I don't. You ought to come and say, "Hey, man, I think you ought to have a little more money." That never happened. I would have to get it myself.

When I come here to Nashville, by the time they'd get through taking out tax and everything, it would run around $84, $85 a week, and I'd bring that check home and lay it down on the table. Now I can bring $5,000 or $6,000 and lay it down on the table, and Evelyn will say, "Where's the rest of it?" Of course, I realize times have changed.

When we were making $90 a week and $18 for Sunday, Flatt would say, "When we were with Monroe, we had to pay our hotel rooms." Well, you could get a hotel room for $2 back then. He said, "He paid us $60 a week." And I said, "Well, that's like $500 now." Later, Bill Monroe would take care of his men with rooms, you know, but Flatt just didn't care. We'd pull up to a place, he'd grab his bag and check into a motel and leave us sitting there.

Kenny Baker and I pay the men good that works with us now. We furnish them a room, and most of the time we pick up the tab on their eats, because we want to treat them like we were never treated.

But I'll have to say this, we was all anxious to get that first bus. I signed the paper.[1] You take six guys staying on there, it gets pretty raunchy, but we had our little stove and everything. There was no time to check in a room. That bus was what I was looking for, because you could lay down and rest. And if you got into a town and did have any time, you could check yourself into a motel if you had the money.

Once the Foggy Mountain Boys were in California for a month, staying on the bus. No place to take a bath, no toilet on there or nothing. Earl flew in and saw how we were being treated. He told Flatt, "These boys will kinker on there . . ."; that was the word he used. I heard them back there getting into it, and Flatt come up to the front then, and he said, "Well, we decided to check you all into a hotel."

All the time Flatt was making out like it was Earl's fault for all these things, and it wasn't. Earl had to get by him. I told my partner the other day, "If I book these dates and get all this legwork done and everything, if anything goes wrong, I'm the son of a bitch. And you're the great guy." And that's the way it was with them, because Earl had to do the hatchet work, is what I called it, and I learned a lot from the ways he did things. He was honest with everybody. There's no more honest man living than Earl Scruggs. If he owes you a dime, he'll walk in the snow and pay you. There's not too many of them left, you know.

I've never seen a woman as smart in business as Earl's wife, Louise. As an agent, Earl would have been one of the best, but he taught her to do that. That's what kept them up there. When I come to work with them, Earl handled everything. He taught Louise these things, you know, like how to handle a booking date.

I remember one time, I hadn't been with them long. That was before he got hurt. We was at WSM studios, and a guy come in and said, "Would you go over to Omaha, Nebraska, for $600?" Just waiting to see who was manager. And Earl said, "No." The guy said, "Just over here to Omaha. Six or seven hundred miles." Earl said, "I said no." He said, "Earl, I said $600." Earl said, "I said no." He wouldn't go for that price. That was his way.

And when he got hurt, he laid up in bed there at home. He had his phone right there, and he booked us. He kept us working every day. Well, Louise is sharp as a tack, and he taught her every tactic that he knew. All that time he was out hurt, he was teaching her.

≫ *The Grand Ole Opry*

I never wanted to come to the *Opry*. That was the last thing in my mind. I always worked up north or up the east coast from Knoxville, and I would have never come to this town with anybody else besides Flatt and Scruggs. I've seen guys who would give you their car to get on the *Grand Ole Opry,* just to say they'd been there one time. And I never did, you know. I loved the old place, but it was more like an old show then than it is now. You went out there, and if you could do it, fine. If you didn't, they'd lead you off.

I've seen some sights there that you wouldn't believe. I've seen shoot-outs right there in that alley; fights outside the old Ryman.[2] One night I come out of there. We was between shows, and this ol' boy said, "I've got a brand new rod and reel. I know you fish a lot, and if you'll come down to my car, I'll give it to you." I said, "OK," and we stepped out in the alley. The ol' boy, he'd parked his car there. You wasn't supposed to be in there, but they wouldn't do too much to an entertainer. We got about halfway down that alley towards Fifth there, and here come these "Pow! Pow! Pow!"— gunshots. I thought at first it was firecrackers.

And here come ol' Curly Harris, a comic with Porter Wagoner. He's going, "Phew! Phew!" like a cowboy, you know, and about that time—"Bing!"— one went right over my head and hit a piece of metal up there, and I said, "Hit the ground. That's bullets, man!"

And I seen this guy run, and he fell right at the steps, right there on Fifth. He'd been into it with a guy across the street in this little beer joint over there, and he pulled out a little .22 pistol, and this guy pulled out a .38, and he was running, and he fell right at them steps. Didn't kill him. But them bullets was hitting everywhere on that wall, all the way around the popcorn machine they had up there.

I'd take off and then come back. In '63 I worked a few dates with Jimmy Martin. I'd left Earl and Lester for a week or so. I believe it was Jimmy's brother-in-law who would invest his money for him in land . . . real estate and stuff. So Martin doesn't have to work in the wintertime at all. He knocks it off about November and won't go back 'til March. He don't want to work but just so much. And I don't blame him for that, really, if he gets the money that he's looking for. No use killing yourself and have to turn around and give it back.[3]

I left Flatt and Scruggs for another short time in about '63. I was just looking around to see if I could find something. Benny Martin[4] told me to call this club in Cincinnati called the Ken-Mill and they'd hire me, and they did, for a heck of a lot more money than Flatt and Scruggs was paying me. So I went in and worked five nights a week with Earl Taylor, Boatwhistle McIntyre, Walter Hensley, and Jim McCall. Man, they had a tough outfit! You didn't work on Sunday or Monday. I'd come home to Nashville, you know.

One night I was there and it was snowing so bad, I wasn't going to go home. Well, this one cat come in there . . . he didn't dig me too much, and he thought I was a smart aleck or something, I don't know. I ain't never been that way in my life, but you know how a drunk will do. And I said, "Well, if you don't appreciate what I'm doing, maybe somebody else does, and if you've got something to say to me after I get through, just bring it outside." Well, he had two or three others there with him.

I went out and I had that Dobro bar in my hand, you know. I didn't ask nobody to go out there with me, but I looked around and there was Boatwhistle. He said, "Well, that'll even the odds a little bit." Here come Earl Taylor. Here come Walter Hensley. Jim McCall didn't come out. But there was a boy there—he'd been learning Dobro—and you talk about a tough little dude. He had a chain, and he knew karate and all this. He said, "All of you just go back in. I'll take care of this situation myself." And, bud, he run them off, and I never was so glad. I wasn't about to run, but, you know, a guy like that, you could get killed. But I'll never forget Boatwhistle. He come right in there. He was a true ol' showman.

You know, a strange thing, I was in Holland, and this guy come up to me and he said, "Do you remember when you worked with Earl Taylor and the Stoney Mountain Boys?" And I said, "Why, yeah." He said, "I've got some tapes of that." And where he got them I don't know. When I come home, he sent me tapes of that old show. I've got them here somewhere. I wouldn't take $1,000 apiece for them. I see ol' Hensley once in a while when I go around Baltimore. He's still picking at some little ol' club. They've been there for years, and they just work the weekends. Jim McCall and Boatwhistle were just small-town boys; they didn't want to tour. They just liked to do the bar scene there, at the Ken-Mill or wherever.

⇒ New Audiences

The perception of hillbillies really bugged me, you know. Even in Carolina, we was "ol' hillbillies." There's more hillbillies in New York State than there are in Tennessee. But, you know, that's the way people felt about us for a long time, and our kind of music—"Them ol' hillbillies." Flatt and Scruggs hated the image. Monroe hated that image, too. All the hillbilly musicians hated the image of being hillbilly, supposedly some ol' boy with overalls on and barefooted, smoking a pipe and got a beard.

Louise and Earl Scruggs turned down the *Andy Griffith Show* because they thought it degraded us, and probably would have at that time. After we broke into that college circuit, they didn't call us hillbillies any more. You don't hear that word hardly anymore: *hillbillies.*

Lester Flatt, you couldn't shake him out there doing emcee. He had a thing about him, the way he could get it over. I remember one time we played Jordan Hall in Boston. Toscanini . . . all the greats . . . had played there. Now, you go to Boston and try to entertain. It's better now than it used to be, but all those uppity-uppity people, you know, were saying, "Well, what in the world is that?"

We looked out, and people were sitting on the stage . . . they couldn't get nobody else in there. And Flatt looked around and said, "I don't know how this is going to go." I said, "Well, there's one way to find out." Lester had ice water in his veins. So we walked out there, and he strummed that guitar one time and said, "Howdy." That crowd just went up—you couldn't hear nothing for five minutes. I timed it. He looked around at me, and he said, "Well, I guess we got 'em now, boys, let's go." We tore that place up. Everything we did was right.

Every one of us was just as country as you can get. I remember we was doing a show at the Paramount Theater on Broadway, and they wanted it to be uppity-uppity, and this guy runs over to Flatt and said, "It's time for makeup." Lester said, "What are you talking about? We don't have to have no makeup." He said, "Oh, you'll die out there under those lights." Flatt said, "Hell, we hunt possums down home in Tennessee with brighter lights than that. I'll tell you what. We'll go out and do it our way. Now if it don't work, then we'll do it your way." We went out there, and they wouldn't let us leave that stage. The guy just shook his head and walked off, because Flatt knew. He didn't want to be something he wasn't. He was careful of that.

We played every major college in the United States and even overseas. That changed the market for bluegrass overnight. When the other acts started getting those colleges, that brought the rest of bluegrass music back. Our first big show for the college audience was at the Newport, Rhode Island, festival in 1960. The first trip to California was '61. Joan Baez was there, and Ramblin' Jack Elliott. Joan Baez, I remember she was driving an old hearse to get around.

➤ Big Money and the Breakup

We was in California working the Ash Grove, and Louise Scruggs was with us. And they was going to do this *Beverly Hillbillies* TV show. Those guys come down, and we didn't know what was going on. We just did our regular thing. They got hold of her, and she wasn't sure she wanted us to do that.

So they brought a pilot episode and showed it down here at the Tennessee Theater in downtown Nashville so we could see. A private showing, just for our families. And as long as it didn't degrade what we was doing, she didn't care. She worked that out, and that made us. We was doing fine, but we jumped from $3,000 a day to $5,000 and $10,000. That makes a difference, you know.

We went in and cut these little spots in *The Beverly Hillbillies*.[5] We didn't know what we was doing. If you listen, I was playing the guitar, not Dobro, on some of the slow stuff. That paid awful good, and then when the TV show came out, it hit like a ton of bricks, and we shot right up there.

When the big money started, that'll ruin anything. If you cut a bluegrass record and you sell ten thousand copies, that is a big hit for you. We were the first bluegrass group to sell a million copies. We did that on "The Ballad of Jed Clampett."

It looked like Earl and Louise Scruggs were taking over the Foggy Mountain Boys, but it had been that way all the time. Flatt didn't worry about the bills or anything. He would just come in and pick up his money. They'd say, "Let's settle up," and he'd say, "Ah, let's do it later." Louise had to take care of all that.

I remember one time Louise negotiated a new recording contract. A new man came in for Columbia Records, and he offered them a deal if we'd do so many Dylan tunes and stuff like that. I know this for a fact, that she got Lester and Earl a guarantee like $45,000 a year apiece—flat money guaranteed whether they sold a record or not. Who else could do that?

And it worked. Maybe we didn't like what we were doing, but it sold to the underground.[6] I'll never forget when that happened, and we had to do all these tunes. Flatt didn't want to do some of them. Some of them was pretty good, and some weren't worth a dang far as I was concerned. "Mr. Tambourine Man," you know, that, to me, is great stuff right there, and we had a good cut on it. But we got a little far out there, and I think it hurt a little bit. Some of it I didn't like to do. I loved Dylan's work, but not all of it. But Louise negotiated a contract for that, if we'd do so many of those tunes, and, man, what are you going to say?

We *had* to do some different stuff, man. We was at a standstill. Wasn't selling nothing. Columbia wanted to pick some tunes for us to do, and Louise signed a good contract with them, and we had to do it. Maybe we didn't want to do some of the stuff, but we had to. I told them, I said, "Why I'd just sit down if I was getting that kind of a guarantee a year. I wouldn't care if I went out anywhere or not. I'd just keep my radio program, television, and *Opry,* you know." But it didn't work out that way.[7]

Part of the hard feelings came from Earl bringing in his son Randy. He was a real musician. Once in a while, he'd also use his older son Gary. Randy used to sit with Lester, teaching him the new songs. Lester never did like it. After awhile the whole band was running scared. Me and Lance LeRoy[8] had the tough job. We had to work with both of them, splitting up the records and things. They were such good friends for a long time—twenty-two years. But I'm going to tell you something: Money will change anybody. Then, too, Earl wanted to help his sons, which I don't blame him for that.

I never could stand some kind of feud or something going on in a group. I'll just get out at the drop of a hat. I always would. I would now if I was working with a group and something like that happened. I just had it all up to here. If you can't go out and play and enjoy yourself, why go out there?

Earl originally came up with the Foggy Mountain Boys name, and he owned it. Flatt sued them for fraud, and that was a slap in the face, because I knew Louise better than that. Flatt wanted the books audited. I told him he wouldn't find anything. The audit cost $5,000, and he wanted Earl to pay half. Everybody always thought Louise was tough and hard. To me she was one of the finest people you'd ever want to meet. Earl and Louise have been awful good to me. They was business, strictly business. If I borrowed $100 out of that company, I had to sign a note, son. And that ain't nothing but business.

Josh's parents, Troy and "Ma" Elizabeth Graves. (Courtesy of Evelyn Graves)

Troy Graves—Josh's father—and Josh. (Courtesy of Evelyn Graves)

Cliff Carlisle, a mentor and influence, in the 1930s. (Courtesy of Country Music Hall of Fame® and Museum)

Lightnin' Hopkins, a mentor and influence, at New Orleans Jazz Fest, 1974. (Courtesy of the Michael P. Smith Collection at the Historic New Orleans Collection)

Josh Graves at the microphone, Jake Tullock playing bass, and Monroe Queener on Dobro at the Cas Walker Show, WROL-AM, Knoxville, Tennessee, late 1940s or early 1950s. (Courtesy of Bobby Wolfe)

Esco Hankins and the Tennesseeans; from left to right, Josh Graves, Esco Hankins, "Kentucky Slim" (Charles Elza), Elizabeth "Aunt Liz" Miles, and Cleve Jones at WLEX in Lexington, Kentucky, around 1950, while they were on the *Kentucky Mountain Barn Dance*. (From the Sonja Davis collection, courtesy of *Bluegrass Unlimited*)

Evelyn Graves and infant son Billy Troy, summer of 1954, Richmond, Virginia. (Courtesy of Evelyn Graves)

Josh Graves and son Billy Troy at the first house in Nashville, probably 1959 or 1960. (Courtesy of Evelyn Graves)

Josh and Evelyn Graves at the Tennessee State Fair, September 21, 1965. (Courtesy of Evelyn Graves)

Wilma Lee and Stoney Cooper and the Clinch Mountain Clan, probably taken at the WWVA Jamboree, Wheeling, West Virginia, in the early 1950s; left to right, Stoney Cooper, Abner Cole, Wilma Lee Cooper, and Josh Graves. (Courtesy of Evelyn Graves)

Josh Graves clowning with another artist's gun belt in Nashua, New Hampshire, while a member of Wilma Lee and Stoney Cooper's band, 1952. (Courtesy of Evelyn Graves)

Charlie Bailey and the Happy Valley Boys, WWVA, Wheeling, West Virginia, 1954. Clockwise from top, Charlie Bailey, Josh Graves, J. D. Maultbay, and Henry Coffey. (Courtesy of *Bluegrass Unlimited*)

From left to right, Josh Graves, Tex Logan, and Mac Wiseman during an appearance of Mac Wiseman and the Country Boys in New England, 1954 or 1955. Tex, a graduate student at MIT, had formerly been a member of Wilma Lee and Stoney Cooper and the Clinch Mountain Clan while Josh was in that band. (Courtesy of Evelyn Graves)

The Foggy Mountain Boys in concert, mid-1950s; from left to right, Curly Seckler, Josh Graves, Paul Warren, unidentified bass player, Lester Flatt, and Earl Scruggs. (Courtesy of Evelyn Graves)

Martha White Mills publicity postcard of the Foggy Mountain Boys in front of their bus, around 1956; from left to right, rear, Lester Flatt and Earl Scruggs; front, "Kentucky Slim" (Charles Elza), Josh Graves, Curly Seckler, Paul Warren, and Onie Wheeler. (Photo: Jeanne Gordon, courtesy of Evelyn Graves)

The Foggy Mountain Boys, around 1960; from left to right, Jake Tullock, Lester Flatt, Josh Graves, Earl Scruggs, Billy Powers, and Paul Warren. (Courtesy of Country Music Hall of Fame® and Museum)

From left to right, Jake Tullock, Josh Graves and "Julie," around 1960. (Courtesy of Evelyn Graves)

From left to right, Josh Graves, Jake Tullock, Paul Warren, and Charlie Nixon, around 1960. In 1972 Nixon replaced Josh on Dobro with Lester Flatt's Nashville Grass. (Photo: William A. Conn, courtesy of Evelyn Graves)

From left to right, Josh Graves, Billy Edwards, and Jimmy Martin during one of Josh's breaks from the Foggy Mountain Boys, February 1963. (Courtesy of Evelyn Graves)

Josh Graves and "Julie" in the den, October 1965. (Photo: Bobby Wolfe)

The Foggy Mountain Boys, around 1966; from left to right, rear, Earl Taylor, Earl Scruggs, Lester Flatt, and Paul Warren; front, Jake Tullock and Josh Graves. (Courtesy of Country Music Hall of Fame® and Museum)

The Foggy Mountain Boys, around 1968; from left to right, Lester Flatt,
Earl Scruggs, Johnny Johnson, Josh Graves, Paul Warren, and Jake Tullock.
(Courtesy of Country Music Hall of Fame® and Museum)

Josh Graves and Lester Flatt, 1968. (Courtesy of Evelyn Graves)

An early live performance by Lester Flatt and the Nashville Grass, 1969, at Shindig in the Barn, Lancaster, Pennsylvania; from left to right, Jake Tullock, Vic Jordan, Josh Graves, Paul Warren, Roland White, and Lester Flatt. (Photo: Artie Rose)

The Nashville Grass at an early bluegrass festival, around 1970; from left to right, Josh Graves, Jake Tullock, and Lester Flatt. (Photo: Ed Huffman, courtesy *Bluegrass Unlimited*)

Josh Graves and Bill Monroe at the Early Bird Bluegrass Concert at the Grand Ole Opry House, October 15, 1975. (Photo: Carl Fleischhauer)

Josh Graves at a Nashville session with Ed Read—his manager—and Columbia Records' Ron Bledsoe, with guitar. (Courtesy of Country Music Hall of Fame® and Museum)

The Earl Scruggs Revue, 1973; clockwise from left around Earl Scruggs, Jody Maphis, Steve Scruggs, Josh Graves, Randy Scruggs, and Gary Scruggs. (Photo: Slick Lawson, courtesy of Scott Lawson and Sony Music Entertainment)

Son Bryan and Josh Graves, from the back cover of Josh's solo album, *Alone at Last,* 1974. (Photo: Bob Krueger, courtesy of Sony Music Entertainment)

Evelyn and Josh Graves, 1980s. (Courtesy of Evelyn Graves)

The Masters promotional shot for CMH Records, 1989; from left to right, Eddie Adcock, Kenny Baker, Josh Graves, and Jesse McReynolds. (Photo: Ken Kim, courtesy of Eddie and Martha Adcock and CMH Records)

Publicity photo of Kenny Baker and Josh Graves holding "Cliff," 1990. (Photo: G. W. Austin, courtesy of Evelyn Graves)

From left to right, Vassar Clements, Marty Stuart, and Josh Graves laugh at Marty's impersonation of Lester Flatt, 1992. (Photo © Dan Loftin)

From left to right, Josh Graves, Earl Scruggs, Vince Gill, and Ricky Skaggs, probably in the late 1990s. (Courtesy of Evelyn Graves)

Kenny Baker and Josh Graves at the River Valley Bluegrass Festival, Ontario, Canada, August 1999. The photo was given to Josh by steel player Anne Werbitsky, who appears at right, flashing the peace sign. Dobro players Jim Crawford and Gord Devries are in the background. (Courtesy of Evelyn Graves)

Josh Graves with "Cliff" and Jerry Douglas, probably in the early 2000s. (Photo: David Wilds, courtesy of Evelyn Graves)

Josh Graves and "Cliff" in the late 1990s. (Photo: Jim McGuire)

Josh Graves and "Cliff" in the late 1990s. (Photo: Jim McGuire)

Josh Graves playing "Cliff" on the "pickin' table" built for him by Eddie Adcock, in the early 2000s; from left to right, Josh, Bryan Graves, and Josh Graves Jr. (Courtesy of Evelyn Graves)

J. D. Crowe and Josh Graves at a bluegrass festival in the early 2000s. (Courtesy of Evelyn Graves)

Josh Graves at his den at home in the early 2000s, with Dobros and awards. (Photo: © Tim Barnwell, www.barnwellphoto.com)

5

1969–1994,
King of the Dobro

After Lester Flatt and Earl Scruggs split in 1969, Josh Graves went on to play with both men in their new bands. Flatt maintained a traditional sound, including several Foggy Mountain Boys in his Nashville Grass and playing many of the former band's classic hits. Flatt stuck with another longtime bluegrass practice: paying his sidemen very little. Graves, one of the most prominent players in the field, was earning $165 a week with Flatt in 1972 and paying his own hotel expenses.

Meanwhile Scruggs, after a break, started working with sons Gary and Randy on new directions that took bluegrass as a starting point but also included rock and pop influences. As a result, Scruggs was operating in a higher-stakes world and paid his men accordingly. They were living the high life, literally, flying to gigs across the country because Scruggs's packed schedule didn't allow for bus travel. Graves's accounts of flying with Scruggs in the pilot seat show a driven side of the man that few saw as clearly as Graves: "I tell you, anything Scruggs started, he'd finish it; if it's picking that banjo or flying that plane."

We get an account of one of the best-known breakups in bluegrass lore: the day Kenny Baker, the longest-lasting Blue Grass Boy, finally left Bill Monroe. Graves also recalls a string of bluegrass feuds involving major stars, such as Flatt and Monroe snubbing former friends for years at a time because of real or perceived slights. Graves was there when behind-the-scenes efforts to get Monroe and Flatt together finally paid off backstage at Bean Blossom in 1971.

Teaming up with Kenny Baker in a long-lasting duo starting in the 1980s, Graves joined another of the most influential and most admired sidemen in the field. Baker's fiddling owed debts to pop and Western swing as well as to bluegrass, a perfect counterpoint to Graves's orientation to bluegrass and the blues.

Earl quit for a time after the breakup. Flatt told me he was going to keep working and asked me if I wanted to. I said, "Yes." So he told me, "Get me a couple of pickers." I contacted Vic Jordan and told him I'd heard he and Roland White were leaving Bill Monroe. If Flatt had known that, he wouldn't have took them. Vic said they were going to Germany for three or four days, but they'd give their notice when they got back. So I just brought them on before Flatt knew what was happening. There was Jake Tullock and Paul Warren from the Foggy Mountain Boys, and later we brought back Johnny Johnson on rhythm guitar. I stayed for about two years before I took out on my own.

Roland and Vic were still there when I left. And Flatt hired Haskel McCormick. He helped drive, and Lester featured him on the Opry. He liked him, you know. There he was with two banjo pickers . . . that's the way he'd do things. Vic left, then Flatt fired Haskel and got Kenny Ingram. But Flatt wouldn't do anything himself.

Lester Flatt had his babyish ways and everything had to be his way, but I could get along with him. I worked for him, and I had another phone put in here. I took care of his business and kept us working. He wouldn't or couldn't go to a guy direct and tell him what he wanted. I'd have to go. With Flatt and Scruggs, Earl was the hatchet man. So that's what I had to be. I had to fire Vic one time. We'd say, "Wear a blue shirt," he'd wear a white one—that kind of thing. We went down to make some publicity pictures, and he turned his back. Flatt called the next morning and said, "Fire him." So I had to. You know, it makes the guys feel bad at you, but what are you going to do? You're getting paid to do that. It's not a pretty thing, but I had to do it.[1]

When I left Lester Flatt, I was making $165 a week, and I was making $25 more than the rest of them were making. God, when you've got a family and you're paying for a house, that ain't no money. He told everybody he was paying me $390 a week. I would have followed it right to the end if he had been. But that's been about twenty years ago. On the road he wouldn't pick up any expenses. No, sir. Just wouldn't do it. If we checked in a hotel, we checked in ourselves. I think he got to paying for that after I left.

Flatt didn't like long-haired hippies. That's what he called them. "Long-haired sons of bitches . . .," that's exactly what he'd say. He recorded this song, "You Can't Tell the Boys from the Girls," and I tried to get him not to sing it around those places, you know. I said, "God almighty, you and Monroe ought to be tickled to death. All those hippies breathed life back into what you was doing." And they did.

When Lester and Earl went out on their own, there was some jealousy there, and they didn't speak for years. Bill Monroe was that way, too. I knew him before that, and when I came in with Flatt and Scruggs, Bill wouldn't speak to me. But the boys in the band talked. They didn't want us to, but we did. James Monroe and Joe Stuart talked a lot with me, and that's how Lester Flatt and the Nashville Grass got booked into the 1971 Bean Blossom festival. I'd go tell Lester good things Bill had said about him, and James would tell Bill the same things about Lester.

When Lester was asking about the June schedule, I told him we were going to Bean Blossom.[2] He said, "You've got to be kidding." That's when Flatt and Monroe sang together for the first time in twenty years.[3] Monroe came in backstage, and he came straight for me and says, "Where's my boy?" and picked me up. Flatt was standing there looking out the window, and Bill just wheeled around and said, "Welcome to Bean Blossom, Lester." It was like they had never left. Monroe said, "Some people want us to do something together." Flatt looked over at him with those beady eyes and said, "Can you still hack it?" Bill said, "We can try it." They walked out there and it happened. When they hit the stage with those old songs, I don't think there was a dry eye.[4]

Lester Flatt was the best rhythm guitar player for our stuff that's ever been. I didn't know how much I would miss him until he was gone. Sometimes I sit here by myself and play those old records just to realize where I come from.

There was a lot of controversy in the Nashville Grass; we got to where we couldn't get along. And I just got tired of hearing it. I got a call from San Francisco to do this album. They paid me a thousand bucks and a plane ticket, and while I was there I recorded with Boz Scaggs and picked up another two or three hundred just overdubbing. And when I come back, I had a session with Charlie McCoy: "Today I Started Loving You Again," which come out about a year after that. They pulled it as a single and made a hit.

When I was working with the Nashville Grass, Flatt knew I was recording with everybody. I told him that was the deal. He said, "Ah, just don't say nothing to nobody about it." But the other guys in the band, they got a little jealous. One time we was coming down the interstate out of Kentucky, pretty close to Christmastime. I'd heard this record and didn't know who it was at first, but it was me with Charlie McCoy. That thing took off like a bullet, you know.[5] I didn't want to make the other guys feel bad, because they couldn't record with nobody. We stopped at this truck stop, and that thing started playing. It was playing when Lester went to the restroom. I said, "Lord, I hope he don't hear that. He'll know that's me."

So a few days later, we'd come out of St. Cloud, Minnesota. I was playing with the kids at home and just in the best humor. Flatt called me, asking what did I mean by laughing behind his back about running around and recording with everybody. I said, "I never done that." Some of them told him I did, you know. "I think you know me pretty well. I wouldn't do something like that." One thing led to another, and I told him what he could do with his job real quick.

From then I didn't know what I was going to do. I just turned in notice and took out on my own. In April of 1972, Kenny Baker and I cut our first album on Puritan. I was working my notice at that time.

The Earl Scruggs Revue

Scruggs had started the Earl Scruggs Revue, and Randy was over here . . . him and my boys was raised up together, all them kids. He walked in, and I was picking something, and he said, "That ain't too bad for an old man." I said, "An unemployed old man."

Randy said, "You're not with Flatt no more?" And I said, "No." He said, "Why don't you call Dad?" I said, "I don't know if I want to do that or not." But anyway, I had to go to town and do something, and when I came back, Earl had called and wanted me to come over and talk to him, and I did. We made a deal, and I stayed with him two years. I made a lot of money with Earl, and he treated me like somebody.

Earl and that bunch forced you to work up new licks. You had to come in there on the stuff they were playing. It was so loud I couldn't hardly stand it, but I really enjoyed it. It opened a lot of doors for me. They were into a lot of things, and we put out a good number of albums.

When I was with Earl, we played to young crowds. And I wouldn't have wanted to play a better audience. I'd get out there and mingle with them. The college kids knew that I was down to earth with them. But it runs like a four-year cycle; they'll get something else, and then it'll come back, maybe. A lot of the acts thought that you could book those colleges like you could a theater. You can't do that. They've got a committee, and they rate you like 1 to 14, on your drawing power. I've never seen Earl rate less than 13. Flatt would go in around 6 or 7, when he started playing again.

After Lester and Earl split, Earl was doing the same old tunes with a little modern touch. Earl got bored with bluegrass—I'll tell you that. He just didn't want to play it anymore. They had that big beat, that sound behind it, and that's what he liked. I know we cut "Bridge Over Troubled Water" and played the same way you would if you was doing it 'grass, but with that big, full sound back there it changed it that much. He'd play "Foggy Mountain Breakdown" with that band and people would go wild.

Everybody said, "Oh, Earl's gone." And I said, "Yeah, to the bank." You talk about rolling in the big bucks—he did! They was making money before they split, but it about tripled. Instead of getting $5,000 or $10,000 a night, he'd get $20,000 or $25,000. We'd be on big shows with James Taylor, Roberta Flack, and people like that. Like the Grateful Dead, we'd do a show for them. That's where the money was at. And you can't do that in 'grass. I love to play 'grass; I still do. But talk about the money, country is where it's at now. Those guys are getting anywhere from $10,000 to $37,500 a night, with the big records.

Earl carried his own sound people and everything. Two drivers. Most of those ol' boys in bluegrass, if they can get them a bus, they'll get one Greyhound wore out twenty years before and they'll fix it up, you know. Some of them you can't even get parts for. Lester and Earl always kept a bus, but they kept it up. You didn't look like a rag going down the road. The night after I left Lester, he bought a new Silver Eagle.

The first year I worked with Earl, we flew everywhere. And you know that gets expensive . . . you've got to be making some money to do that. But we was making such jumps that we couldn't have made it by bus, no way. We might be here today and Denver in the morning and Seattle or someplace. Then he bought this Eagle. I said, "Man, I'd rather have this." You've got your clothes on there. You don't have to jump from an airport, and if you're there one night you've still got your stuff on the bus, you don't have to keep moving it. And I really enjoyed it. The beds on there are just like home. That suited me fine.

I'll tell you what Earl did do. . . . I remember one tour was like Seattle, Washington, to Portland, Oregon, then right down to California. He sent the drivers on to meet us in Seattle when we got through and then take the bus on the rest of the trip. Then we'd catch a plane in Los Angeles, and those boys would drive the bus back. And that made it nice, you know.

Earl put a pickup on his banjo. I was the only one playing acoustic in the bunch, and I couldn't hear nothing. Full drums and everything was so loud, you didn't even know what you was playing. I'd come off the stage, and my ears would ring for ten minutes and I couldn't hear nothing.

I'd had a few offers around, but I just sat here one night. We'd come in off the road. I got into that Scotch pretty heavy, and I said, "Well, I'm going to tell him." I called Louise, and I asked her who I turned my notice in to, her or Earl. She said, "I guess Earl." I said, "I'll be over there in a few minutes." I went over and I told him, and he wished me well. He knew I was trying to do something for myself. And I got the nicest letter from him, you know, saying he wished me well in anything I did and he appreciated me working for him.

I've got all kinds of clothes I bought when I was with Earl. Everything but hats. Earl hates hats, but I'll tell you I need one. The sound bounces right up on it. Even Kenny Baker will say I can't play without my hat.

⤳ *Flying with Earl Scruggs*

Earl was a pilot. I'd go with him when he was learning to fly. That was in, I guess, '57. Jake[6] and I still lived in trailers over on Dickerson Road, and he'd want me to go with him. Earl's wife and kids would stay with Evelyn, and me and him would go. Flatt was strictly against flying. All of them was but me. I said, "Man, let him go. That's something he loves." And it fascinated me. I was the first passenger he ever had, and I wanted to learn, too, but then it was like ten bucks an hour to learn to fly.

In the late '50s, me and him would go to the John C. Tune airport over in Bordeaux, north of Nashville. I'd go with him and sit there, watching the planes come in, whatever, and he'd go up with the instructor. I forget how long that run.

One time we was in Jackson, Mississippi, and he was ready to fly solo. I was eating a hamburger at a little ol' snack bar while the instructor took him up. They came back and handed him his permit. Earl said, "Do you want to take a ride?" I said, "I might as well. I've been with you this far." The guy said, "Do you want me to hold your hamburger for you?" I said, "I may not be back. Just forget it." He took me up, and it didn't scare me at all.

Then we'd go on these show dates, and he'd fly from Nashville to wherever we was going—Arkansas or something—and I'd ride back. I wanted to get home, you know. I never was afraid of flying with Earl. He checked that plane. . . . Of course, just like a car, it can still quit on you.

I remember one time we flew to Knoxville. We were doing a TV show and coming back home. Me and him stayed all night. He didn't like to fly at night until he got his instrument rating, and he didn't have radar on that plane. And in that valley there it would get so foggy, and he wasn't flying that high. Now coming through the Cumberlands . . . he was afraid of those mountains in a small plane. He said, "If it don't clear up in just a little bit, I'm going back to McGhee Tyson Airport in Alcoa." I said, "Whatever you want to do." Then all of a sudden he looked down and he seen the interstate, and he said, "We're all right." And he followed the interstate right home.

One night after the show, he said, "Do you want to fly with me?" And I said, "Yeah." I had a pint of vodka. I'd killed about half of it before I got on that plane. I never had flew of a night. We were coming back out of Arkansas, and he'd do anything for a little joke. I looked down, and I seen these little lights shining, and I said, "What is that down there, Scruggs?" He said, "It's either Tulsa or Little Rock." I said, "You don't know?" I killed the rest of that pint, you know. But he was just putting me on.

One time when I was in the Earl Scruggs Revue, he was going to buy a DC-3. And we was going to try it out. He had a pilot that went with him, most of the time anyway. We was going to Ruston, Louisiana, and there was a squall line reaching all the way down that way, and I didn't know this. Gil Ferguson was the pilot. He was an Army pilot, a good pilot.

But anyway, we got down there. Gil almost flipped it. He almost hit the mud before we hit the pavement, he told me later. It stormed all the way down there and back, and everybody was sick but me. They had couches and everything on there. I couldn't get up to go to the bar, it was pitching so bad.

Coming back, we was right over Memphis. Wasn't flying too high—not high enough we had to have oxygen. Me and Vassar Clements were sitting there playing cards. Something hit that plane, man, just like a truck run into us. It scared the hell out of me. Vassar liked to bit the end off his pipe.

Gil come back in a few minutes and said, "Hope that didn't disturb you-all." He said, "I slammed a door up front here, and I guess you heard that." I said, "Ferguson, don't you lie to me. You hit something." He said, "I'll tell you about it later." When we got to Berry Field,[7] where we landed, there was blood all over that plane. We hit a flock of geese flying at 5,500 feet. Can you imagine that? I didn't think them things got that high. I said, "I knew that you didn't slam no door. I knew we hit something." If it had hit a little farther, it'd knocked that whole windshield out. But he was a good pilot.

I loved to be around those guys and listen at them talk. It was something I'd never get to do; it fascinated me. It still does. Earl taught me a lot of things. He's a good pilot. But he still hung one out here at Cornelia Fort Airpark a few years back.[8]

I was sitting here one morning, and it flashed on the news, "Earl Scruggs in an Airplane Crash." I dropped my fork. He'd been working at Paris, Tennessee, or somewhere over there. It ain't 150 miles, you know. They took the bus and he flew. They told him to come in at Cornelia Fort if he could see. And evidently about that time, right on that Cumberland River, the fog come in and, man, he lost it. He caught that fence when he went over. He had his landing gear down. He completely demolished that plane, and it throwed him out.

He laid out there for five hours. Nobody knew nothing. They'd turned the landing lights on over at the airport, but they didn't know what was going on. And they just turned them off, I guess. Randy went out there searching for him, and he heard somebody hollering, "Help, help!" It was ol' Earl laying down there in that field. He'd broke his left wrist, broke his nose, and broke his ankle. Well, immediately, when I heard that, I called at the house and they said, "Yeah, it's true, he did." I said, "Could I go see him now, do you think?" They said, "Yeah, just don't mention nothing about the rig."

I didn't want to excite him, just see if he's all right. But they had him in his cast and everything by the time I got up there. I was going to brighten it up a little bit, and I walked in and there was the ol' feller laid with his arm up like this and his leg and that nose that big. I said, "Chief, you look better than I've seen you in a while." But he survived that just like he survived the car wreck. The car wreck was a hell of a lot worse than the plane crash.

One winter, we had to go to Chicago. It was the awfulest snow you've ever seen. We couldn't get there with the bus. And the airlines wasn't going in. Trains were stopped. But he had that twin-engine Apache. So here we go. And the plane in front of us crashed. Skidded off the runway. But he took her right in there. And we went in and made our date. The cab driver didn't want to take us down to the college, but he found out who we was, and he was from the South, and he took us. The looters was breaking in trucks and everything, just taking what they wanted. And they had no food in there. There was another snowstorm coming in, so we left early. Earl got us out of there.

I tell you, anything Scruggs started, he'd finish it, if it's picking that banjo or flying that plane.

⇗ Kenny Baker and Josh Graves

Me and Kenny Baker teamed up in 1984 and are still doing it.[9] We've had a good run. We've made some money. Everybody said, "Well, that won't last three months." It's been nine years and still going.

Kenny's got a style all his own. I've never seen a smoother fiddler. They respect him now for his playing. Earl Scruggs always plays a tune exactly the same way. Kenny Baker cannot. Baker plays it differently every time. So do I. If you'll notice, I always change it.

Bill Monroe and Kenny Baker got into it when Kenny left. It had been coming for a long time. Kenny didn't want to go with them to Japan. If you've got a family, you want them to know where you're at in case something happens, and you need an itinerary, you know, to leave with them. Say there's a death in the family and they've got to get hold of you. My father-in-law died when I was overseas, and they didn't get the message to me for two weeks.

Kenny asked for an itinerary, and they kept dragging their feet and they didn't give it to him. They was working Jamison, Alabama, and Monroe said something to him on the stage that was real hot, and Baker . . . I don't care where he's at—if he's in church—the way he feels about it, that's what he'll tell you. They'd done all them tunes, you know, and then somebody asked for "Jerusalem Ridge." Monroe looked around at Kenny, sweat rolling off him, and said, "Do you want to do that 'Jerusalem Ridge'?" And he said, "Not particularly." And it made Monroe mad, and he turned around and he said, "Well, you'll never play it on my show again." Baker said, "That's fine." Just held up his fiddle to the audience and walked off the stage.

The audience didn't know what was happening. Bill come onto the bus and they got into it, and I guess there was some words exchanged you couldn't print. But then they brought him the itinerary down there to go to Japan, and he wouldn't take it. I didn't know this was going on, see. One day somebody called me and said, "Did you know Baker left Monroe?" And I said, "You've got to be kidding." I didn't know what had happened. It wasn't none of my business.

He'd do that every once in a while, but it wasn't on that account.[10] But, anyway, I was going up to Kentucky to do an album there with some people, and they needed a fiddler. I said, "Maybe I can get Kenny. He's not working with Bill." But in the meantime, we'd done two albums together, just me and him.[11]

I called him—I finally got his number. They wouldn't give it to me out at Bill's office, but I got it from one of his friends. I called him and said, "You want to go up into Kentucky and pick up a few dollars, if you're not doing anything?" He said, "Why, yeah, I'd be glad to." So I picked him up and I called him and asked if he'd work another date over in Carolina, and he said, "Why, yeah." I picked him on up and we done it. It went over so good that I asked him, "Well, what are you going to do?" He'd been working some with Bob Black and Al Murphy. They was out at Iowa, up in there. They had some dates already booked. I said, "Well, if you want to do some things, let me know," and he said, "Well, yeah, be glad to." So I started setting up a few things around what he already had with Al and Bob.

One Sunday I invited Bill Monroe to go to church over here where I go, and he came. My wife, kids, and I went out and had dinner with him. And I said . . . I always called him Mr. Bill . . . I said, "Mr. Bill, now you know that me and Kenny's doing a few things together." And he said, "Yeah." I said, "I just want you to know that we didn't plan it." He said, "I know you better than that. I know you wouldn't do that." I said, "You know we done those albums together. That was just a thing that they wanted us to do, and the thing took off like a wild hare."

Once Kenny and I were doing OK together, Bill wouldn't speak to me again. That's strange. James hired me to go up to Bean Blossom with him to do his show—I used to do a lot of work for James, when I wasn't doing anything else. I got up there . . . I was just as happy as a lark because I didn't have nothing to do with that deal between Baker and him. Bill come up on the stage to sing with James, and I spoke to him and he wouldn't even speak.

They have what they call a Sundown Jam, and I was there right beside of him. He'd usually call me up first one. He just ignored me, and he brought every Dobro picker they had up there but me. I turned around to James and said, "The hell with this noise. I'm getting out of here." I just went over and put my guitar in the case, because I was working for James, you know.

When me and Kenny Baker started together, Bill Monroe didn't speak to us for about eight years. Me and Bill speak now; he called me on my birthday. Our friendship goes back a long way.

Bill Monroe was bitter, and I don't know why. If you were my friend and you'd worked for me for twenty years and you said, "I'm going to leave," I'd say, "I hate to see you go. I hope you do well, and if there's any way I can help you, I'll do that." But that's jealousy in bluegrass music, and there it is.

Flatt was that way, too. You left him, buddy, and he wouldn't speak to you. Oh, man, he didn't speak to me for the two years I was with Earl. And tried to hurt me every way he could. He tried to cut me down at the banks, you know. Told them I was leaving town and they better watch me, and all that stuff.

Jake Tullock had left him, too. He was up in East Tennessee working at the police department. He called me one morning. That was the maddest little rascal you ever seen. He said, "What's this I hear about you and Evelyn getting a divorce?" I said, "What?" He said Lester Flatt had told him me and Evelyn were getting a divorce. I said, "Well, I don't reckon. She's sitting here. I'll let you talk to her." You talk about a mad woman! And little things like that.

One time up in Renfro Valley, Kentucky, my friends were there, and they hollered and said, "Where's Josh?" Flatt said, "He died." I sent word to his manager, "If I hear that one more time, somebody is going to hand him a little piece of paper, and he knows what that means." Because that hurts you, you know, around. But after I left Earl, everything was just cool. That's baby stuff. Like Bill and Lester and Earl, they didn't speak for twenty-two years.

Martin Haerle of CMH Records and my son Billy Troy got together on the idea of the Masters. Kenny Baker, Jesse McReynolds, Eddie Adcock, and I all knew each other, so we just went in there and done it. CMH is pushing it and an outfit in Los Angeles is starting to book us tours.

I keep me and Kenny Baker working. Earl and Louise Scruggs taught me a lot of things about booking. I can tell them to go to hell in two minutes, just like Louise could. I do it a little bit different. I let them think they can do me a deal. You can't con a con man, you know. I'll tell them what I've got, and if they want to buy it, fine. If they don't, they don't.

I was on this fiddle tour in the '80s with Kenny Baker, Alison Krauss, and a bunch of other fiddlers from different kinds of music.[12] I played the bass with Alison and all the rest of them, and then I'd go back on Dobro with Kenny. I enjoyed that so much. My finger was sore . . . oh, man, it was sore. I played the bass on square dances when I was a kid. Blood would be running out of my finger. But then finally when that callus came on there,[13] man, I could stand there all night.

We play a place now—Hiltons, Virginia, the Carter Fold—and every third tune you've got to do a fiddle tune or up-tempo tune where they can dance. I do that and imagine how it was back about the time I started. Everybody would go on Saturday night for a square dance. And they still do a lot of that in Virginia, West Virginia, and Kentucky—the eastern part. I thoroughly enjoyed those square dances, but it would nearly kill the fiddlers, standing up there.

I try to copy Lester Flatt's way of handling a show. I don't bore them to death; I just say a few words. If I'm going to do a little comedy bit, I pull it on Kenny and go on with it. There's a lot of people don't know how to do that. You've got to study it and think, "How am I going to get away with this little joke here? Will I hurt anybody's feelings?"

In California at Grass Valley, in this little bit that I pulled on Kenny, I said that the doctor told him he had to lose 120 pounds of ugly fat, so he went home and run his wife off. Just a joke, but this woman jumped all over me, and she kept on and she made me mad, and then I told her husband he'd better get her away from me. But, you know, I wouldn't do nothing to hurt nobody's feelings in that audience. I try not to do that.

I had this heart problem about four years ago and had a valve replaced, and I do a little takeoff on that. I say, "They put a government heart in there, and I know it was, because I went home and signed up on welfare and ain't worked since. When I had my operation, they told me they'd put any kind of valve I wanted in there, either a pig valve or a metal valve. I said, 'Which one is best?' They said, 'The metal one.' So I said, 'Well, get the metal one and don't get it to rust too much.'" I say, "I can't tell too much difference in it. My Uncle John had the same operation, but he had the pig valve put in. And he can't tell no difference in it either, only he runs around grunting every day at the house and wants to eat off the floor." Just little ol' things like that . . . it gets their attention.

I'll walk that floor and shake hands with people when they come in the door, and I'll be there when they go out, shaking hands with them, thanking them for coming. That's how I built up a following for Kenny and my show. Our fans find out where we're going to be and pack the place.

6

A Man of Many Talents

For country and bluegrass stars from Hank Williams to Bill Monroe, songwriting was a key part of what it meant to be an artist and a professional. Almost all the early bluegrass stars were prolific composers, thereby increasing their incomes as well as expressing their thoughts of love and loss, home and travel. Josh Graves was very much of that school, turning out songs and tunes that endure in the classic repertoire. Stars often got a piece of the song for recording it, and the names Lester Flatt, Earl Scruggs, and their wives' maiden names appear on some of Graves's copyrights. But he was able to avoid a common occurrence of the day: selling off all rights to a song for a fraction of what it would eventually earn.

In addition to performing and writing, Graves had to make sure he had a loud, well-set-up instrument at all times. Commonly known by its earliest trade name, the Dobro is a six-string guitar with an internal resonator to increase volume and strings raised off the neck to allow them to be fretted with a metal bar. Graves played several different original Dobros as well as modern resonator guitars and a vintage Regal-brand instrument he called "Cliff," after his mentor Cliff Carlisle, who had previously owned it. In this chapter Graves reveals some technical details, including the kind of metal bar, picks, and strings he favors.

Graves's unique marriage of the blues and bluegrass created a brand new sound for the Dobro that kept him busy for years as a studio musician, bringing his originality to many other artists' recordings. That meant he had to adapt to new musicians and styles virtually every day, while retaining his distinctive sound and achieving the high levels of musical quality that session work demands. True to his creative nature, he came up with something new for every take.

Graves's optimistic personality and storytelling ability also served him well when he went out as a solo artist, sometimes with his sons, but often with pickup bands whose quality could vary widely from town to town. In the unrelenting pressure of travel and performance, Graves admits to developing a taste for alcohol, but he didn't give in to other drugs he encountered in the growing counterculture. As he notes, someone must have been looking out for him in a long and successful career.

⤳ Composer of Songs and Tunes

I used to write a lot. "Come Walk with Me" did real well. I ended up paying a lot of old bills with that song. Actually I wrote it for Benny Martin. I sat right here at this table when we lived at Four Way, me and Evelyn; she helped me with it. I wrote it on a piece of brown sack paper. Curly Seckler and I sang it for Lester, and he just walked off. Benny played the fiddle on Wilma Lee and Stoney's cut, one of the biggest records they ever had.[1]

I was riding home from doing radio shows downtown, and me and Flatt had the radio on. Here came "Come Walk with Me"—Benny kicking it off: dit-de-diddle-de-diddle-de-diddle-de-DAH. Lester said, "Goddamn, that's a beautiful song!" And I said, "Well, thank you." He said, "What do you mean?" I said, "I wrote that song." Oh man, he just hit the ceiling. "Why didn't you bring that to us?" I said, "I did. You laughed at it." I had to tell him about Curly and me singing it for him.

Well, they had a thing out of New York at that time, the Top Ten Tunes—country, whatever. And it broke in about number 8. Flatt came by, and he said, "I'll give you $250 for that song."[2] I said, "No, I'm with that like I am with a dog. I wouldn't sell that song." And here come Earl two weeks later. It had moved up to number 4. He said, "It looks like you got you one. Do you want to sell it?" I said, "No"—and I needed the money. He said, "I'll give you $500 for it." I said, "I'll tell you like I told Lester. I brought it to him and he laughed at it. I let Stoney do it."

I tried to give Stoney part of it to do it. He said, "If a song is good enough to do, I'll do it, and you don't owe me nothing." Well, the thing kept coming up them charts. A big Cadillac pulled up one Sunday morning. Here's Stoney. He wrote me a check for $1,000. Said, "I want to buy 'Come Walk with Me.'" I said, "It ain't for sale, Stoney. But I'll still do what

I told you I'd do. I'll give you half of it." He said, "No." I tore his check up, and I throwed it in the ashtray. Junior Huskey[3] called me and said, "You didn't sell that song, did you?" And I said, "Not today." He filled me in on the money I'd have coming in from that thing. The others knew; I was just a little dumb.

I remember me and Evelyn had been to the store, and we come back, and we'd been into it about something. I said, "Well, check the damn mail over there." She said, "There's a little piece of paper in there." Well, it was a certified letter, and they couldn't leave it. I said, "Well, that mailman is coming down the other side of the street. Give that to him and he'll give it to you." There was $2,300 in the letter. Whew! I said, "Damn, I wish I hadn't told you to get it. I'd have went and got it for myself."

I've got a lot of good songs. I can't understand why somebody other than Flatt and Scruggs ain't picked up "Someone You Have Forgotten." I wrote that song in Virginia. Mac Wiseman cut one of mine, "Now That You Have Me (You Don't Want Me)." That's been thirty years ago. I ain't never drawed one dime off of it. I'm going to do it again and put it with another company. Recently some of us heard the Appalachian Grass do "If You're Ever Going to Love Me,"[4] and someone said it was a real pretty song, and I said, "Thank you."

I just don't have time to write anymore. If I go up in the mountains at home, I might sit around and write some. I need to be alone. I just get an idea and go from there. I don't have to work hard at it.

I've got 137 songs recorded. And about one hundred of them, Flatt and Scruggs had to have their name on, when they didn't have any more to do with them than nothing. You'll see "Stacey—Certain—Graves." That was Louise Scruggs's and Gladys Flatt's maiden names, and that goes back to a contract Lester and Earl had with a publishing company. They had to put all their material under those names. Back there in those days, they took part of your tune, and if you didn't do that it'd lay there. And I thought, "Well, a third is better than nothing."

I made some money from those songs but missed out on the recognition. Ricky Skaggs, Jerry Douglas, and Tony Rice did "Fireball" live with J. D. Crowe and the New South, and it won a Grammy.[5] Jerry brought me a certificate out here as a writer of "Fireball" and gave it to me. He said, "I think you deserve that." He knew.

≫ Dobro Master

I'd always wanted an original Dobro, but coming up I couldn't afford one. I didn't know what it was, really. I didn't even know what to ask for, but I'd seen them, you know. The first good one I got was in 1947. An ol' boy hocked it to me for eight bucks he was needing to make his car payment. He said, "I'll get it back to you in two weeks." So he came back in about three weeks and said, "Do you want that guitar?" And I said, "Why, yeah, man." He said, "Just keep it for what I owe you." I said, "You've got to be kidding!" And that was one of the best ones I ever had.

That was my first real Dobro. I played it until I went with Wilma Lee and Stoney. Sold it in Canada. Then I got a fourteen-fret and played it while I was with them and Mac Wiseman and Toby Stroud. I cut "Randy Lynn Rag" with it and then sold that one in Canada, too.

A fellow up in Johnstown, Pennsylvania, wrote me and wanted $100 for a Dobro. I guess it was in '56. I told him to send me a picture or I would give $70 for it sight unseen. He sent me a colored picture and said I could have it for the $70. He shipped it to me. An old friend of mine, he's a black man, had a gun that he carried all the time. He called it "Julie." I fished with him all the time. So when I got that guitar, I just named it "Julie." I've had "Julie" a long time. Sold it once to a friend in Texas. He kept it a year and gave it back to me. Said it belonged to me.

"Julie" was gone three years. Stolen at a Loew's theater in Syracuse, New York. I was there with the Earl Scruggs Revue. We had a picture session, and I even thought about this being a good time for it to get picked up. I looked around, and it was gone. We reported it, and three years later, Earl got a call from a girl who was mad at her boyfriend, and she told him about it. We found out it was still in Syracuse. Cost me $350 in expenses sending two friends after it. The police got involved, and, rather than prosecuting, I got all my expenses paid and got "Julie" back. So I was satisfied.

I like a good bassy sound, and I don't like a shrill pitch. I like one that will carry. If you hit it and it dies, look out. A lot of them will sound pretty up close, but I've got to have something on the stage that'll whack it. Early on with Flatt and Scruggs, we just used one mic. With six of us, you had to have something to cut it. Nothing is going to cut a banjo, but "Julie" came as close as any I've ever seen.

I used an R. Q. Jones for a while. Jerry Douglas had to buy his, and I didn't. They called me and asked me if they could fix him one. I said, "Well, yeah, I don't have nothing against that." I used my R. Q. Jones for two or three years. Something happened to mine. I sent it back, and it never did sound right again. I sold it.

Same way with the Reed guitar. See, Bob Reed was the one that made the guitars for Rudy Jones.[6] He made a fine guitar. He bought Jones out and started his own company. I used one of them for a long time. We were in Holland and staying at this apartment, and I had the guitar laying out. We'd been rehearsing, and this boy's wife fell off a stool putting up some curtains and squashed it, and I sold it over there.

But I don't think any of them is built as good as this Beard, that new one I just got. The wood's got a lot to do with it. A year from now, you wouldn't think it was the same guitar. You play it all the time, play the sound into it. If you ever watched a Gibson guitar back in the old days, that shellac or whatever was on there, when it started cracking just a little bit, that's when you had a beautiful sound. And a Dobro is the same way; it's got to breathe.

Now this guitar, it's mahogany. When that lacquer or whatever is on there starts to break up, then you'll hear the difference. You take a fiddle and you put it up for a month and it won't sound the same. After not picking a Dobro for a long time, it will go dead. I'll take mine out of the case and set it close to the stereo or TV to keep the vibrations going. Here, we'll leave it on all the time. You can sit close to it, you know, and you'll tell the difference. Sure will.

Maybe I'm old-fashioned, but I think the age of the wood's got a heck of a lot to do with it. My "Cliff" was made in 1929, and it's seasoned; it's there, you know. Cliff Carlisle's folks gave it to me after he died. I turned down $5,000 for "Julie" and a heck of a lot more than that for "Cliff."

It takes a lot of hard work to get started. But it is like swimming or bicycle riding; you never forget it. I might run over a couple of tunes before going on, but I don't have any particular practice habits.

With so many younger fellows and different styles, you'd better stay on top of it. You've got to work at it. I used to do tapes for Tut Taylor when he was learning to play, and he took that flat pick and he'd go around like Jesse McReynolds on the mandolin, and he mastered it pretty well.

I never did much with retunings. I started tuned to A, but I didn't like the shrill pitch. I was kind of like Jerry Byrd with that. Somebody asked him why he didn't put pedals on his electric steel. He said, "Show me where I can eat better putting them on there and I'll do it." Oh, I experimented sitting here at my table. I used to sit here at four in the morning learning new riffs.

I like my strings set wide at the bridge. You need them wide to do the rolls. My strings are .018, .018, .026 (unwound), .036, .048, and .058. I used the Gibson 248 for years; they quit making them. I'm using John Pearse now. They last and last. At first they had a wrapped third. They're making mine now with a plain third. I've never had a set time for changing strings. They usually get good about the time the wrapping wears out. I've seen people use everything to bring them back: buttermilk, hot towels. . . . Norman Blake taught me on the hot towels. That does brighten them up for a while. I change strings one by one, so I don't have any problems with buzzing or getting it to sound right again.

When I was with Esco Hankins, I used an old flat bar, a learner's bar with those little crosses in there.[7] About '49 I went to a Stevens bar. I used National picks and later switched to Dunlops. We played so much, I've had hands just bleed because the picks were cutting in. New strings cut the brown thumb picks bad, not so bad on the white ones. Sometimes I'll use rosin to keep my thumb pick on in the summertime.

A lot of musicians capo, but I think it kills the true sound of the Dobro. I very seldom use a capo. Just maybe when I go out with Jimmy Martin or I'm recording and want to play a roll on open strings. Flatt would turn over in his grave had he any way of knowing I was using a capo on that guitar. But I do use it once in a while. Kenny Baker plays a lot in B-flat; you can't play those fiddle tunes if you're just clamping down chords. But I don't like the capo. Now Jerry Douglas can use a capo. The rest of them, they'll play the same chords they'd play if they didn't have the capo. All they're trying to get is the open strings.

The bone nut that Bobby Wolfe put on "Cliff" works fine. I've got an old Stevens Trutone nut raiser I've used for a hundred years. I've tried everything for a bridge, but I go right back to maple.

I've always liked the old stamped cones in the old Dobros, but I've used Quartermans and I liked them. There's one in "Cliff" now. I considered putting a poinsettia cover plate on "Julie," but I never did. I said, "What am I doing? I'll just get more ashes in it." I prefer the standard cover.

Onstage, if you're lucky you'll get a Sony pencil mic. They work awful good. Usually you just have to use what's there. I've been accused of electrifying my Dobro, but I never did. I did an album with a song called "Uncle Josh Plays 'Lectrified Dobro,"[8] but it was only reverb. I've got cussed out for that more times than I care to remember.

➢ *Session Musician*

In the year after I left the Nashville Grass, I made more money recording with different artists than I did with Flatt in the previous year. I guess I've cut session work with about all of them. I've even cut some rock stuff with different groups. For five years, staying in the studio was about all I did. I wouldn't want to do that all the time. It would drive me crazy to be there day after day. I'd rather a group go in and do their thing and leave me a spot and I'll fill in. Playing backup, I just try to hit between lines or at the end of a line. I don't try to crowd them; I try to do something that will match up with it but not cover them up. I don't like to see a lead man go right in on top of a singer.

In five or six takes on a tune, every time the guy might sing it the same way, the fiddle player might play it the same way, but I never play it the same way twice. Somebody'll say, "Damn it, Josh, do it like you did it before. I like the way you did it." I'll just say, "Well, you'll want the other take, then."

It runs in a fad, you know. For about five years, I stayed in the studio. I cut with everybody, even with Boots Randolph. But it'll slack off. They'll come up with another sound; they'll hear that, and then they'll change. Only thing was, back when I hit it, we wasn't making the money then. Just like ballplayers, they wasn't making the money back yonder that they are now. Don Drysdale and Sandy Koufax was holding out for $115,000 a year, and they had a heck of a time getting signed. But look at it now—millions. It's about the same in this. I hope Jerry Douglas is taking advantage of it. If you're lucky enough to get in on that train, take advantage of it. Because there'll be one day that you won't. Yes, sir.

I've always said if you heard one of my records, it will sound pretty much the same in a concert. I just don't believe in doctoring it up. One of my favorites was the Cotton Town Jubilee album that me and Jake Tullock cut in 1963.[9] I used Oswald Kirby, Chubby Wise, Curtis McPeake, and others.[10] That thing's a collector's item. It was selling for $300 in Europe. Then it was reissued.

I don't like to listen to recordings I've made. It's kind of like a little kid shying away from something. I think to myself, "Well, I've done it. If I've made a mistake, I don't want to hear it." I believe I've made about twenty-five or twenty-six albums in my own name, a lot of them out of print.

⮞ *Solo Artist*

I worked about every college in the United States when I was playing with Scruggs and the Revue. Then when I broke out on my own, I did the same thing again. The first year I broke out,[11] I made $87,000 and I thought I was in clover, but I've been lucky ever since then.

These new groups go out there with a program glued to the back of their guitar. They got to follow that, you know. I never do that. I never know what I'm going to do. I just go out and play whatever suits my fancy. If I get in a bind, I know I can do something else.

Guy come up one night, and he said, "Hey, Josh, do ol' 'Don't Let Your Deal Go Down.'" I said, "Lord God, man. I ain't done that since I left Lester." He held out his hand like this, and he reached it to me, and I held out my hand and there was a $50 bill in it, and I said, "I just remembered that thing." I played it for him twice that night. They do some of the strangest things if they like you.

Something I never could understand was a group working a club for a kitty.[12] I would never let that happen to me. You never know what promoter is sitting out there watching you who'd think, "Well, I can get them for nothing." It's all right if somebody comes up and hands you a ten or a twenty or something, that's fine. But you won't see a kitty in front of my stage. I think it cheapens you so much.

You know that those people have heard of you or they wouldn't be there. They know what you can do in the way of picking. Any of your tunes that you do, they'll like it. So I just keep it off balance, and I do anything. My boy, Billy Troy, says, "Old man, you scare me to death. I never know what you're going to do out there." I say, "That makes a good show because nobody knows. But if you've got some good pickers, they'll jump right in with you anyway and play what you're going to play."

At some festivals the promoter will say, "Boy, we've got you a good group," and then you get there and nobody can play. You can get mad, but you hold it in. It's not those guys' fault, and I don't think you should jump on them right there. I go to the management and say, "This ain't worth a damn. I want to change this." But I've never been one to criticize any of them to their face. I say, "Boy, that was a good job."

Billy says, "You've got more nerve than anybody I've ever seen. You can take a band you've never played with and go out there and do a show." And I can; but I won't put nothing hard on them if I'm picking up a band. He said, "I couldn't do that." I said, "Yes, you could, if you'd just stop and think. Because all of them knows the stuff that we're going to do; they've heard it so many times."

Billy gets mad at me on the stage. I just play the way I want to play. I don't rush nothing. I just let it fall the way it will. What he don't understand is I know them people. I know what they like. He'll say, "Put some pep in it." I'll say, "I do. I do when I want to." But people, even now, they love to hear me play waltzes and things like that. And some of them love to hear me talk, and I can do that.

But I won't let a show drag. I'll keep building it back up, you know. It takes a lot of nerve to go out there by yourself. I'll say, "Well, glad to be here," whatever, "and I'm going to try to do this thing." Nothing fancy. Playing on the sympathy of the audience is what you're doing, really. And they say, "Well, that ol' boy's sincere in what he's doing up there."

It's just like what I said. If something ain't broke, don't fix it. Now I can play the wild stuff if I want to, but I have no reason to. They'd say, "What's wrong with him? Changing after all these years." I go out there and play the "Great Speckled Bird," and people know what I'm playing. I won't do nothing fancy, just what I've always done. If you call blues licks "fancy," I guess I am. . . . I do throw some blues in there.

⇒ Philosophy, Alcohol, and Belief

Lightnin' Hopkins was one of my idols. Blues man. I got to know him real well. B. B. King is about the closest thing to the old stuff you can find today. But Hopkins was so different. He wore sunglasses all the time and had two gold teeth, and he carried his own private bar with him, a little portable thing. Every time I'd go in a club to see him, or I was going through that town, he'd tell them to bring that bar over and give me some good whiskey. He didn't want me drinking that bar whiskey. He was just a great ol' fellow, and he believed in what he was playing. I could sit for hours and listen to his records, and I still do.

Old guys like Lightnin' Hopkins and Son House used a bottleneck and an old guitar. Their singing and picking shows that they came up hard. You watch them on the stage. A blues man will get to just a certain note, and you can tell by the way his head moves what he's doing. He shakes his head and closes them eyes, and you can tell exactly which way he's going. Everybody else that's tried to learn that instrument has tried to play the notes. But they don't have the experience, you know—they don't have the trouble and all the hard stuff.

When I'm doing my shows, I like to do one gospel tune especially. I like to do that for the old people out there, and I just love to do it. But I won't do over two. . . . If I did I'd have to go out there and take up a collection, you know.

I don't believe in going out on your show dead drunk. But I think that any musician you find—a good fiddler, a good singer, Dobro picker, whatever—he's going to hit that booze if he stays in it long enough. Of course, I've got three boys. . . . They've been working a long time, and they won't drink. I guess they've seen me do enough of it, they turned against it.

I was talking to Doyle Lawson. He said a thing up there at Owensboro[13] that made sense. I respect Doyle because he's religious and he don't fool with booze or nothing, and I had a beer in my hand and a cup. I said, "Oh, you caught me." He said, "Let me tell you something. It's not what goes in a man, it's what comes out." And that's about true, you know. You take some of them, they get a few drinks, they go crazy. But if I get too much, I go lay down somewhere. I won't bother nobody.

I don't drink the hard stuff anymore, but if you're out at a party somewhere and you're sitting there while everybody else is boozing it up, you feel, "What the hell am I doing here?" And after awhile you join in with them. But it's a bad thing, and I know it is. Well, I'd rather see that than dope, really.

I was so naive with dope when I first started working those colleges. I've got a problem with a bad stomach, and they wouldn't let me drink anything for six weeks. I was at this party out in California. Somebody said, "Josh, you want a drink?" I said, "No, I can't drink anything." He said,

"How about a beer?" I said, "No." He said, "Do you mind if we have coke?" I said, "No, I don't mind." So they had this glass here and they'd roll up them dollar bills and they was sniffing that cocaine. I said, "Whoa, let me out of here!" But after they found out that I wouldn't take that, when I'd go to one of them parties they'd be smoking a joint and they'd say, "Pass Uncle; don't offer that to him. It'll make him mad." I'll reach back and get my Scotch and hit me a lick. But I just never did take up that dope, and I'm glad that I didn't, really.

Every time that I walk in this door here at the house, even before Mother[14] gets up and lets me in, I say, "Thank you, Lord, for one more trip, for letting me come back one more time." Every time I walk in that door. And I've always come back. Maybe one day I won't. I'm a pretty religious man deep down. I know somebody was watching over me all that time. I've been so fortunate. I've been in three bad wrecks and walked away from them. There's somebody up there looking over me.

Reflections on Bluegrass Old and New

There's a touch of the curmudgeon in Josh Graves as he talks about the old days, the way he and the other founders did it back then. The "classic" bands would often play at breathtaking speeds and push or slightly accelerate certain phrases for added excitement and the elusive "drive" that Graves references. Modern players, he says, go for way-out or eccentric licks that might impress other musicians but lack the heart and aggressiveness that should continue to characterize the best bluegrass. "You just don't hear anybody can cut it that way anymore," he says.

For all his issues with modern bluegrass, Graves served as a mentor to countless younger players, even agreeing to "bless" their instruments when asked. Graves developed lasting mutual admiration and friendship with Jerry Douglas, the young Ohio picker who transformed the Dobro all over again when he emerged in the 1970s to inherit Josh Graves's mantle as "top dog" on the instrument.

Graves was hit hard by illness toward the end of his life, undergoing amputation of both legs, but he continued to pick, joke, and entertain nonetheless. It's fortunate to have Uncle Josh's story in his own words—full of mountain wisdom, the friendships and jealousies of the bluegrass world, and the music that made it all worthwhile. In some ways, he reminds us of Hamlet's beloved and trusted friend Horatio. Born poor before he became a scholar, Shakespeare tells us, Horatio was a friend to the best and brightest, present at every important moment and a survivor who outlived the mighty and dying to tell the story: "Let me speak to the yet unknowing world, how these things came about . . ."

The thing somebody always wonders is where did the term *bluegrass music* come from? How could you get bluegrass music out of Lester Flatt and Earl Scruggs? Scruggs was from North Carolina, and Flatt, Paul, Jake, and I were from East Tennessee. But what happened on that deal is Bill Monroe had the Blue Grass Boys, and he'd always say "the music that I invented." But if it hadn't been for Flatt and Scruggs, there wouldn't have been that sound. It's stuff that we grew up with in those mountains, Earl, me, and Lester. How in the world can you get "bluegrass music" out of a guy from North Carolina and four from Tennessee? It don't matter to me. As long as I make a living, I don't care what they call it, as long as it pays me at the end of the week. But it is strange the way that happened.

If you want to know the truth about it, I think Monroe learned a lot of rhythm from Scruggs. Because Charlie and Bill[1] had the worst timing in the world. They'd start out a hymn in a slow tempo, and by the time they ended it was a breakdown. I don't call that good rhythm; if it was good rhythm, you'd hold it right in that one level. Just forget what everybody else has ever said. Just get the records and listen to the tunes that's on them.[2]

I ran into Charlie Monroe once and asked him if Lester Flatt really played the mandolin for him, and he said, "Yes, he did. Yes, he did." Well Charlie had been talking about his eyes being bad, so I told him not only couldn't he see, he couldn't hear either. Flatt told me he carried the mandolin for $5 extra a week. He could make a few chords on it, but he couldn't really play. His wife, Gladys, was a good singer. They were working in a mill somewhere, and Charlie picked them up. There's an album with her and Lester.[3] I can understand him playing mandolin if they paid him $5 extra. He loved money.

I've known Bill Monroe for a long time, even as far back as Wilma Lee and Stoney. We used to visit and go out to dinner. I've fox hunted with him, and, yes, I've picked with him many times. I've gone out and sat in on his shows. He was quoted as saying the Dobro wasn't a bluegrass instrument.[4] He came to me and told me he was misquoted, that he'd said it wasn't bluegrass unless Josh played it. Bill loved those blues licks.[5]

Flatt and Scruggs broke out on their own in '48. At that time it was Jimmy Shumate, Cedric Rainwater, Lester, and Earl. "Foggy Mountain

Breakdown" came out in '49. And anywhere you go to this day, they'll ask for "Foggy Mountain Breakdown." I'll do a thing on the stage when I play that tune. I'll say, "Our father who art in Nashville wrote this. Earl didn't write too many tunes . . . and after he wrote this one he didn't have to write many more." If I had the royalties off that one song, I wouldn't be here right now. I'd be right up in Tellico with a big villa.

I was with Scruggs when they presented him a plaque for a million dollars in sales on that instruction book he had, *Earl Scruggs and the Five String Banjo*. We was playing in Central Park, New York, when Peer International gave it to him. He's still selling it, you know. If I had the money he made off selling banjos, man, I'd buy Barry Willis[6] one of them jets and just get him to fly me around.

⟫ Modern Developments in Bluegrass

These younger guys coming up, they just don't know what it is. They like Michael Jackson or something like that, which I guess is all right if you like that kind of stuff. I come back home sometimes so confused about what's going on out there. I sit down with Flatt and Scruggs records and listen to what I did. Then I know where I'm coming from again. That may sound crazy, but I think you should go back once in awhile and check it out.

There are individuals out there who are magnificent on their instruments but who don't know the history of the music. They don't care. All they're interested in is that dollar they are going to make or how good they are in pleasing their fellow musicians.

You take a bunch of guys, they get out there and hit these licks, and I won't mention no names, but they play to musicians. Musicians don't buy your records; they expect you to give it to them. You'll see them on the stage. They'll go out and hit the wildest stuff and look around and see if anybody backstage is watching them. That never did influence me at all. I didn't care. I go out to do what I've got to do, and I do it.

Some of those guys . . . if Monroe did it in one key, they'll try to move it up one, try to get above him. And you listen to some of them, and it sounds that way, too. I always hated B-flat . . . it takes quality, I think, out of your instrument. Playing the Dobro up in higher keys kills the sound for me. You notice Flatt and Scruggs, it was like G, C, and D. Once in a while maybe an A, that wasn't too bad.

Back in '88 or '89, Carl Sauceman[7] and I were standing in the area where the artists would be selling records and stuff, and there was a band on there. It was Redwing or something like that. He said something to the effect that, "That music's the same as we were playing forty years ago. They haven't changed the tune. Nothing new." I guess they just worshipped Flatt and Scruggs.

You can't get back to the original thing. They'd have to feel the same way they felt then and play like they did then. Even if you could put them all together, bring Jake back and Lester back and stand them up right now, it wouldn't be like it was then.

But very seldom on these festivals that you go to now has it got the drive like we had in those days. Like "Sally Goodin," they've got to put a minor in that, or "Dusty Miller," or things like that. We never did that. And they think that changes it so much. I was doing this TV show the other day—I can't think of what it was—and this guy said, "You want the minor in there?" I said, "There's no minor goes in that tune." "Well, I'm used to. . . ." And I said, "Play it the way I tell you to. There's no minor there."

This one guy I had to back up was doing "Gotta Travel On," that old Billy Grammer tune,[8] and I'd never heard it done that way in my life. He'd go to A-minor, back to D, and then to G instead of going straight into C, and it sounded good, really—it was different! I said, "Where in the world did you come up with something like that?" He said, "Well, I figured if Mac Wiseman could do it, I could do it." I said, "Well, you did." But you take a lot of those guys, they won't find all that stuff—minors. They say you can't make a minor on a Dobro,[9] but you can.

What I think is guys like me and Kenny Baker, we can still go ahead and do the old stuff, but these younger boys are trying to change it. I don't think they have the ability to drive it like we did. If you get four or five young guys together, everybody's got a different idea. But when you worked for somebody like Flatt and Scruggs or Bill Monroe, you had to do what they told you to do. So that got to be the way of things back then. If you did it wrong, they'd get on your case.

We just stuck it out for that stretch, then when we broke out on our own we could do what we wanted to. But still playing the same stuff. These boys can't play it. They can do the progressive stuff, but they can't do the old hard drive. I can get away with it because of who I am and what I've done—the people expect that. Ralph Stanley's the same way; he can still do it, too.

You see these groups now, and they say, "Boy, that's fast!" I'll play you some tapes of what we did in the old days if you think that's fast. After Lester and Earl split up, Kenny Baker was working with Bill and I'd already left Flatt. Paul Warren got sick and couldn't make it to the *Opry* one night. Lester asked Bill if he could use Kenny on the fiddle, and Bill said, "Well, I guess, if it'll help out." Kenny said, "I went out there . . . they was halfway through a tune before I even got my bow up, they was that fast!" Kenny Ingram on the banjo, you know, "McKinley's Gone" and stuff like that. You just don't hear anybody can cut it that way anymore.

The younger guys, they don't know it. They think they do, but they don't. If you spend as many hours as I have sitting and studying that stuff, you'll know what I'm talking about. You go to some of these shows and you watch it. I've been so bored, I've got so I won't even go out and watch a group anymore, because I get mad with the fact that they don't put any drive in it. Maybe I'm getting senile now.

I'll tell you who's got a good group is Doyle Lawson and Quicksilver. They do a lot of gospel, but they've got a drive to it. Solid . . . yes, sir! And he believes in what he's doing. And it's got to be right, and I think that's wonderful to do. Doyle's been around a long time; I was so tickled when he made it to the top. You just won't beat him. And that drive he's got comes from Flatt and Scruggs. Go on Doyle's bus, you'll see the tapes . . . he plays them all the time. He's got a banjo picker, Jim Mills. He does a good, driving banjo. What I call a clear, clean sound.

I don't go for this chromatic stuff, you know. If I'm going to listen, I'd rather have a Scruggs-type banjo and a fiddle and a plain ol' Dobro guitar I can sit down and listen to. Very seldom do I go out and listen to a group, but I'll go out and listen to Doyle. He's trying to do it exactly like what we had in mind to do, and there's not too many of them left that do that.

You see a bunch of guys now and they've got to have fifteen mics out there. I remember when I started picking we had one microphone, and you could fold the PA setup and put it in the trunk of your car. We'd play those big auditoriums in North Carolina—nine thousand seats— and you could still hear just as good because we had to learn how to do that.

Now I think that's what took away from good picking, all that equipment. You just don't have the true sound. It goes back to ol' Jimmie Rodgers's day. There wasn't a PA setup then. He'd go out and hang his leg across a chair and pick. But in those auditoriums they could hear him. He just did his regular thing. Women'd just go crazy, you know.

I went out to do a TV show this past weekend. They kept asking me if I wanted this or if I wanted that. I said, "Now look, if it's wrong I'll tell you. And whatever you want me to do, you tell me, and if I don't like it I'll sure as hell tell you." They said, "God, man, you're so easy to get along with." I said, "What's the use of giving you trouble?"

Today you don't never see a comic or nothing on a country show. It's just one song right after the other. Now what I'll do is break it up—tell a little joke or something—and keep switching it around and make a little show out of it, instead of just standing there boring them. I guess those musicians who don't entertain feel that it's really not necessary. And it does take a special kind of talent to be an emcee, to do comedy, jokes, or just tell stories.

I know a lot of groups who go on the stage and never say a word from the time they start 'til the time they quit. Then they introduce everybody and leave. You can do that, but I don't like it. I think the people sitting out there paying their money should be entertained, and I try to do that. If you can break them up one time, you've got it made.

When I came to Nashville in 1955, Flatt and Scruggs had the record "I'm Going to Sleep with One Eye Open." WSM banned it on the radio. Can you imagine? There wasn't nothing vulgar about that. It's changed so much now. But I do think they go too far today. Like cussing on a record, I don't believe in that. It's like a comic on the stage. I don't believe you have to get filthy.

I walked out of the Exit/In down here in Nashville one night. I had to listen to this comic. And it was so filthy, I helped my wife up and got almost to the door and he started on me. "Why don't you stay? It'll get better after awhile." I said, "It might, but I won't be here to hear it, and I'll see you again sometime." And I will. I'll recognize him. I never was so insulted in my life. That woman right there means more to me than anything in this world, and I won't put up with that around her. I've had guys come here to the house and they start their filthy talk and everything . . . I'll ask them to leave. That's how funny I am.

I have some grandkids going to school up the street here. They want me to come up and do a show for them. My daughter insisted that I do. And 80 percent are black children, and they don't understand bluegrass music like we would. No disrespect against them. I don't mean it that way. But they're used to blues and rock, you know.

So I called John Hartford, and I said, "I don't know how you feel about this, but I'd like for you to go up to where a couple of my grandchildren are going to school and do a little show. Would you like to do that?" He said, "Why sure, I'd be glad to." And I knew with the comedy stuff that he does, he'd get to them kids. When we went in and took our instruments out, they knew what a banjo was. But they wanted to know if that was a bass fiddle or a mandolin that I was playing.

John tore into that crowd, and he entertained them kids for about an hour. He did that old thing about the washing machine.[10] And every one of them little kids, you could see them going around imitating him when we was leaving. I said, "You started something here."

John Hartford will come and help you, I don't care where you're at. He was awful good through Earl's tragedy with Louise.[11] He stayed right there. He canceled a thing in Owensboro.

That's one thing about a lot of them musicians, you'll find. When it comes right down to it, they all stick together. Like a brother and sister fighting . . . you better not jump in. They'll come and help you any way they can. It's like a bond between pickers. That's the way it is. Like carnival people, they're the same way. I used to follow the carnival, you know, and do shows.

We have a trust fund here.[12] And maybe somebody that we don't even know needs help. Somebody will say so-and-so over here is about to lose his place or his bills are piling up and he's sick. They'll get together, two or three of them, and they'll go to the trust fund board. They'll write him a check. I think it's a great thing.

It's like the IBMA up there. That's going to be a wonderful organization. I was a little leery of it at first, I don't mind telling you. And I told them that. But they're building a fund to help guys that need help. And I think that's wonderful. We've also got the Opry Trust Fund. That will include our bluegrass pickers, because we paid into it just like the country people have.

We finally got a chart in *Billboard* to chart bluegrass records, and some of these disc jockeys won't play them. They're ashamed to, and that's the truth. You've got stations that will in North Carolina, Virginia, and places like that. Even in Pennsylvania. The IBMA finally got the bluegrass chart, and I think that somebody ought to consider that. Like that convention up there . . . that's a big thing, and it's going to get bigger than anything down here, you watch and see if I ain't right.[13] But I think they at least ought to acknowledge some of the talent.

You have a lot of jealousy in bluegrass music, more so than in country. If you'll look around you'll notice that. I think, for many years, bluegrass pickers lived in a world all their own. When it comes to their playing, they'll get jealous of one group over here somewhere. Just seems like one don't want to see the other get ahead, and they'll try to cut another group's throat to get a gig. You don't see that in country music.

I don't know anybody that I've hurt in this business. I think there's room out there for everybody to make a living. If they'd all stick together instead of pulling apart, it'd be a lot better.

You'll hear about these banjo pickers, and a guy will say, "Oh, this guy over here is good as Scruggs." And I'll say, "Bring him on; I want to hear him." All they're playing is exactly what they've heard Earl play. Or a fiddler will copy Kenny Baker, or a Dobro player me.

I played this show the other night, and the little group that was on before me played every one of my tunes that I feature. When they said, "You're on in a few minutes," I said, "What am I going to play?" They said, "Well, he's doing a tribute to you," and I said, "He should have told me about it. I could have made other plans." Of course, I've got enough tunes it wouldn't matter, but they think they're doing you an honor going out and doing your tunes. They don't know they're tearing up your show. It's crazy. I've seen them go out in front of Flatt and Scruggs and do every feature tune that they did before we came out.

I remember one time we was in Louisiana and there were seven Dobro pickers there, and they played every one of my tunes. Flatt said, "What are you going to play?" I said, "What's left to play? I don't know." They do it just to honor you, I guess, but that's all they know, what they've copied off a record. I try to write my own stuff, most of it, and that way if they learn it, fine, let them go out and do it.

I'll tell you, if I get out with a bunch of kids and they want to go along, I'll never do one thing to put them down. But if they try to cut me, then it's like an old boxer that knows where it's at. I'll take it from there.

My friend Gil Stewart told me one time, he said, "Why do you teach all these things?" I said, "Just because I want to." That goes back to Cliff

Carlisle . . . he had time for everybody. Gil said, "Ah, they'll beat you at your own game." But they cannot beat you at your own game.

Sometimes they'll come up and say, "Would you bless my guitar?" The first time that happened, I didn't know what they was talking about. They'd open the case and want me to put my hand on it. I said, "Well, yeah, I'll do that." But it is embarrassing. You don't know what to do or say. But things like that are what make this business so interesting.

I think a lot of Dobro players are trying to create something on their own, based on what they learned from me. I know they have good intentions, and I'm glad to see that, really. I'm proud of what the other players have done. Dobro trends change; there's always somebody coming up with something new.

I never do other players' stuff because, if I do, they'll say I'm copying them. I've got my own thing, and I just stay with that. What I do has never let me down. I never want to change, really, just add to what I'm doing . . . put a little more on it.

What I did kind of caught on, and these days just about every bluegrass band you see has got a Dobro in it. Me and Kenny Baker was over in Holland and Belgium. I did a radio program. I wrote a tune called "Evelina" many years ago, and they'd been using that for a theme for sixteen years, so I had to do it live. I think I did it better than the cut on the record. But anyway, they brought up the subject of progressive bluegrass and how I felt about it. I said, "Well, I guess you've got to change with the times," and you do.

I said, "This young guy Jerry Douglas is coming on, God bless him. He's one of my best friends, and he's a genius when he plays. A lot of these young boys copy him. I had my time, and he's got his. It don't bother me a bit, but they've got to remember to go back to the basics of where it started from." The guy said, "I've never thought of it like that." I said, "Well, think about it. It's like Kenny with a fiddle. If you think bluegrass fiddle, you think Kenny Baker. We're making a living at it, and if something ain't broke, don't fix it. I feel pretty lucky to have done what I've done."

Jerry Douglas can play pretty stuff when he wants to. When he started out, he did my style, and he'll tell you himself he wanted to add something to it, which he did. I love Jerry. I met him when he was twelve years old, sitting around a campfire. He came and listened to me play. It was up east in Ottawa, Ohio. His dad and mother'd bring him to the festivals. We've been friends all that time. He's gone on to fancier stuff, but, I'll tell you, he's a genius. He can do everything. He can play it straight or whatever he wants to. He's a fine fellow and not stuck up.

You hear a lot of this stuff about, "Oh, he's mad at so-and-so." Jerry Douglas and Mike Auldridge, we've been friends ever since they started. I remember one time they had a write-up in *Frets* magazine about different styles and what-all, and Mike and Jerry was talking, and I used a phrase like out of the old West, "I'm like a fast gun, everybody's trying to beat it." And the guy says, "Well, Mike and Jerry's not looking for no shootout, but Graves wouldn't care." Because I'm just going to do what I'm going to do, and they are, too. Just whoever comes out. It might be me.

There's so many young kids coming on now, they get one record and they think they're going to keep on staying up there. You don't see that happen anymore. Ernest Tubb and guys like that, they were a standard draw and they stayed up there for a hundred years. But the old guys in the business, they studied that music—ways to get by and how to please their audience—I think, more than they do today. And that's kind of like in my case. I survived.

One of the things I'd change in this business is education. There was this kid come by here the other day, he's a grandson of a good friend of mine, and he said, "Can you get through to Chet Atkins?" And I said, "Yeah. I'll write a little note and you take it." The boy could pick, but the first thing Chet said was, "Get your education first, and then you learn the hard way." And I thought that said it all right there.

I went to the first year of high school, and I thought I knew more than they did. But it didn't take too much education to play that Dobro. I've seen a lot of times where if I'd went on and got an education, I'd have changed a few things. I see now a lot of things that come up. For example, you're talking to big business people and you don't understand what they're saying. I'll say, "Hold it, just give it to me in plain English, then I can understand what you're saying." I lucked out, but a lot of people won't be that lucky.

8

A Family Musical Legacy

Nothing seemed to mean more to Graves and his wife, Evelyn, than daughter Linda, granddaughter Bambi (whom they reared), and three sons who also became involved in music: Josh Jr., Billy Troy, and Bryan. Even during their inevitable teenage rebellion, the sons found a way to praise Flatt and Scruggs's sound in comparison to other bluegrass acts, saying "it didn't sound like someone cutting a pig." They learned music from their dad by osmosis, it seems, but also got heaping helpings of road smarts, using Josh's network of friends, fans, and acquaintances when they started their own road careers.

Lest anyone think that bluegrass arose in simpler, gentler times, a few sample stories of Graves's wild and reckless relatives will set the record straight. His formative musical experiences took place in a time when violence and poverty roved through the mountains like a fiddler through the bands.

As his musings wind down, Graves sounds as though he's trying to answer one of the enduring questions in this kind of music: To play it right, do you have to come from one of the Appalachian states, have to have grown up on a farm or in a small town, or know how to build a lean-to if you get lost in a snowy forest? He doesn't sound as doctrinaire on the subject as some people on the question of "true vine" versus city players, but he does offer one memorable thought: "It helps if you're raised in the mountains."

☞ *A Proud Father, Uncle, and Grandfather*

Evelyn and I raised some of the finest musicians, I believe, in this part of the country. That sounds like a father bragging. I ain't got one that'll take a drink. I ain't got one that'll smoke. I wonder where they got that from? I've done everything in my life. I've been wilder than a March hare. I never got on dope or nothing like that, but I'd drink any whiskey or beer or whatever, and if you said, "Let's go to California," I'd go with you. But I'd always come right back.

I guess I'm funny about my boys. I never taught them to play. Didn't want to. Lester asked me one time, "How do you get your boys to play guitar?" I said, "I tell them, 'Don't touch that instrument.'" I knew how I was when I was a kid.

I've got a son that plays country. I've got one that does rock. And I've got one that does bluegrass. Now, we have some discussions sometimes, but I never knock any kind of music. I don't care. I've got one grandson who loves the clarinet and Bach and all that stuff. He was ashamed to tell me, afraid I'd jump on him about it. I said, "Son, listen, that's my favorite kind of stuff to sit and listen to," and it is. So it don't matter to me.

Good kids . . . can't beat them. I'll have to say that. I'm proud. Now we get into it, son, listen . . . I'll invite them out in the yard. I still will. I'm sixty-five years old. Well, you know, I never would take anything. I was brought up proud and guess I'll die that way. If you lose that pride, you ain't got nothing. I guess we was so poor growing up—mountain kids—we learned things like togetherness.

Two of my sons are having a little controversy now; they can't get along. I said, "I'll do you like my Uncle Bud did his boys." They couldn't get along; they was drinking and all this, and he said, "Next time you come around like that, I'll fix you." A couple of weeks went by and they done it again. He lined every one of them up and shot them in their ankles. He got their attention. My cousin told me, "I picked buckshot out of my ankles for three months." But he never had no more problems.

You know, my boys coming up, they'd listen to Flatt and Scruggs. They said it didn't sound like somebody cutting a pig. And if you'll notice, our stuff was down in a moderate range. You didn't have to strain so much to get to it.

Billy Troy's real name is William Troy Graves. Named after his two grandpas. He never wanted to go by "Graves." He said, "I don't want to ride off of you. If I can't make it on my own, I don't want to do it." Bryan goes by Bryan Angel with the group he had. I respect them boys for that. My third son's Burkett Jr. Boy, you call him Burkett and he'll fight you . . . he's a cop, you know.

You see a Merle Haggard Jr. out here and you see Buck Owens Jr. and all that. But my sons did not want to do that. I say, "Well, it's there. If you want to use the name, go ahead and do it. I don't know how much good it'll do you." But they've found out in the last few years. Say one of them breaks down in some town. He'll call me and I'll say, "Well, I've got a friend that lives there." They'll say, "Are you kidding?"

Bryan's van broke down not too long ago up in Ohio. I said, "Wait right where you're at and I'll have somebody call you. This guy's a Dobro picker, and he's one of the best mechanics you've ever seen." He went out and got it and fixed it for me for $175. If it had been anybody else, it would have cost me five or six hundred . . . the whole rear end, differential, everything in there. Bryan said, "I don't know how in the world you do it." And I said, "I'll tell you why, because I've made friends everywhere I go."

My brother-in-law said one time, "That little sawed-off so-and-so can go from the East Coast to the West Coast and never cost him a nickel." And I could. I've got friends all along the way. If you was coming through this town, you'd say, "Well, I'd better call Josh." And that's exactly the way I do it. When I get into a town—if I'm flying—if I've got an old friend, I say, "Hey, man, I'm at the airport. Don't want to disturb you or nothing, but I'll be here for an hour and that's about all I've got, but I just wanted to call and say 'hey.'"

These people who fixed Bryan's van put him up for about three days at their house. Of course, that just suited them because they love music and Bryan played the bass while they sat there and picked. They'd go out and get pizza and whatever, and saved me a ton of money.

Like, they're going to Louisiana, I say, "Well, let's see now, which way are you going?" They know I know everybody on the route. "I've got a friend in Enterprise, Mississippi, and all down through there. If you should have a breakdown or something, give them a call." Kenny Baker's a little funny. He don't like going to people's houses. But like, this boy that fixed the van . . . if I'm going through there and I've got a day or so to kill, I'll go stay with him. I've got my own room. In Enterprise it's the same. And if I go through North Carolina, it's the same thing.

CMH Records came to me one time and wanted to do a Graves family album. But I couldn't get my boys all together to agree on everything, and I said, "Aw, to hell with it." I just forgot about it. Billy's recording today, I think, somewhere. Bryan is a good road man. We never have to worry about nothing being set up. They're always there. He helps drive and sets up the sound system.

I've got a nephew—Tim Graves—I love him to death, taught him to play Dobro. I'd come home and give him a week's worth to work on. When I came back, I expected it to be there. I can hear him on the *Opry* out here. He works with Wilma Lee, and if he hits it wrong I'm going to call him the next day and say, "Come over here, I want to talk to you." And it has sure helped him to know that somebody cares enough to correct him.

A lot of the tunes, Tim would say, "I can't play that." I say, "Take a stab at it. Try it. If it comes out wrong, it comes out wrong. It's better than standing there looking." Maybe I've got the wrong idea about it, but I don't think I have.

I've got another Dobro player coming: a grandson, Billy's son. He's coming along.

⮞ *Home in the Mountains*

Tellico Plains don't change much there. It's just a little mountain town. I think the population is thirty-five hundred, something like that. And the main industry there was Stokeley's canning factory. They'd have a plant there to can beans and kraut. Another place it would be tomatoes and so and so. They raised a lot of cabbage there, too. For years and years, that was the main thing, you know. About all my uncles worked there at one time or another. And after that thing went out, about ten years ago, there's nothing there now. People just live there, and if they work, they work in Madisonville or Sweetwater, Tennessee. It is about fifteen miles to Madisonville and about fifteen more to Sweetwater.

I still have some people who live in them mountains; I'm proud of them. They won't take nothing off of nobody, no outsider. They live in a world all their own. They hunt and they trap and they fish, and whatever they want to do. They just want to be let alone. I go up there and I sit down and listen to what I call "them old residenters" that knew my daddy and my uncles.

My Uncle Bud in Monroe County, Tennessee, was a real mean man, and he'd shoot you in a New York second. He didn't bother anybody. But if you got on him, look out. I was up there in the mountains, and a friend of mine that runs this motel, he was telling me about meeting him. They'd never seen my Uncle Bud. One night they was out coon hunting, and they had one in a hole there that they was trying to get out, and Uncle Bud walked up. They had their lanterns. They said, "Could we borrow your gloves to reach in there and get that coon?" He said, "Hell, no, you can't borrow my gloves. Get your own gloves." They said that was the meanest looking man you ever seen in your life, about six foot tall and he wore overalls. He carried a .30-.30 rifle over his arm all the time. He'd go into town and he carried it.

My Uncle Bud was killed there. He was going home one evening from the Stokeley canning factory, and some boys had broken into his house. They knew they'd have to kill Uncle Bud or he'd get them. He was walking home, him and his youngest boy, and they shot him in the back. Four times.

My Uncle Jake up there, I never seen him but one time. This guy was running around with his wife. Jake went to him and told him he knew about it. He said, "Now, I know what's going on, and if you want to knock it off right now, that's fine. If you don't, you'll answer to me." And he said, "No, Mr. Graves, no sir. It'll never happen again." About three months later it started up again.

One day, my daddy and another one of his brothers came across the mountain. They walked everywhere they went; they didn't have no cars. And they seen these buzzards circling around. They thought somebody drug a cow or horse off up there. And up under these bushes here's this raincoat—a slicker is what they called it—and they uncovered this guy my uncle had been into it with. He met him up on that mountain. He'd done warned him, you know. He shot him in two with a 12-gauge shotgun.

Then they had to go tell the sheriff. My uncle got so mad at them, he was going to go after his own two brothers. They had to get out of town 'til things cooled off. The law went to him, and he told them, "Yeah, I killed him. And I'd do it again, if I could." So they gave him thirty, forty years in prison. It was on the North Carolina side, Butner Prison. My daddy always felt guilty about that, and he'd take him tobacco and clothes.

Uncle Jake did his time and didn't have nowhere to go. Outside, where would he go after all them years? Daddy couldn't take him home with him, so he stayed on there and worked in the hospital until he died. My daddy shipped his body back to their hometown and buried him there. He's buried right by my daddy and my mother. But you wouldn't call that being mean. That'd be called somebody who just didn't take nothing, who stood up for what he believed in. I respected my uncles for what they believed in.

Now on my mother's side—the Thomases—it was altogether different. They was all religious people. My grandmother Thomas, she was a little tiny woman. She'd come and visit us, and I'd haul her around in my little wagon. She couldn't read or write. I was old enough to go to school. I could read, you know—and I'd pull her, hitch my belt and get a string and tie it to that wagon tongue, and I'd pull her out through the fields and I'd read the Bible to her, best I could read. I loved her so much, but my other grandmother hated me.

Grandmother Graves lived to be 103 years old. She was full-blooded Cherokee Indian. The boys would sit down at the table when they'd all gather there, and I'd be there. They'd say, "Reach that jug down there." An old jug with a corncob in it that's full of whiskey, a gallon of whiskey in that thing. They'd say, "Reach it down to mammy. Let her have a drink." She'd take a drink right with them. My hair was coal black—I took after my mama's people—and all the Graves were kind of sandy-headed. And she always said I wasn't a Graves because my hair was black; that'd just make me so mad—I was a little ol' kid.

She was a deal, man. Listen. There wasn't a hospital back there that I ever knew. She fell and broke her hip one time, and it growed back, I guess, the best way it could. They were just mountain people. I couldn't figure out what they was doing. I did later.

I don't know of any other place I'd rather go for a vacation, really. I've spent a lot of time in Louisiana, but in the summer it's so hot down there I can't stand it. October is always real pretty up there. Tellico Plains is the wild boar capital of the world. They have hunts there every October. A couple of my cousins and one of my uncles were guides in the mountains. There's some good fishing up there, I tell you, that trout fishing.

I love to go and just stay a week or so and just get away from everything. But people find out I'm there, and they'll be there, you know. And they'll aggravate you if you ain't careful.

I got snowbound up in the mountains up home a few years back before my brother died. I'd go up there to stay two days and stay two weeks, you know. These ol' boys I went with was crazy . . . we grew up together. They had some of these torpedo peppers, they're so hot; they come from Mexico. We'd get us a jug of that white lightning and eat those hot peppers, and they would burn you up.

This little Dobro picker found out I was down there. He was from Knoxville . . . that's forty-eight miles away. That snow was coming in. I didn't care, of course. Oh brother, he loved picking. He couldn't play a thing, but he was sure a backer of me. The boys I was with called him aside and said, "Now, if you want to play like him, you've got to eat them hot peppers like Josh eats."

In a little while, I looked around, and he was about to die. He'd eat half of one and have to lay it down. He couldn't go no farther, you know. It liked to killed him. But that snow came in, and he got out of them mountains some way or another, and I've never seen him since. He probably don't want to ever see me, but that wasn't my doing.

That's the worst place for copperhead snakes you've ever seen. I remember one time I was walking up that river road. I was just a little feller going, and never looked down. My brother hit me and knocked me out of the way. I was ready to come back and fight him. There laid that snake in the road. I'd have stepped on it if he hadn't done it.

And one time we was picking huckleberries—big ol' things—you can make wine with them. And what I didn't know I had to learn the hard way, that a snake will lay right by them bushes where them berries are at and the birds will come in, and that snake will pop them. We was going up through there, me and my brother Dick, picking them huckleberries. All of a sudden he hit me, knocked me down, plumb away from that bush. I was ready to fight him again. There laid a rattlesnake, already coiled. And he taught me, from then on, to look for snakes. If the sun is shining, you'll see them eyes glittering, you know.

A copperhead is just about the same color as the ground. You've got to watch them. That's the deadliest one. But a rattler, he'll hit that rattle, well, and at least he'll let you know that he's there before he hits you. But a copperhead won't do that. We have things here called a pilot snake. They go in front of a rattlesnake and they rattle just like a rattler. And they're not a bit poisonous. But, in August, when they can't see—that's the old story—they go in front of those rattlesnakes. And here, if you see one you know the other one's right there close.

I used to hunt out near here—this ol' man named it Josh Mountain— out between here and Hendersonville or Gallatin. I'd go up there and he had hogs running. Now if there's hogs in a place you're hunting, you don't have to worry because they'll kill every snake they find. One day I went out there, and they'd moved those hogs. And my son Billy Troy was with me; I had him on my back. It was still warm . . . you know, the season opens too early here. I heard that rattler start. And of course Billy didn't know what was going on. And I just froze until I could hear exactly what direction he was; he was in front of me. I knew he wasn't behind me, and I backed down that mountain, with Billy on my back.

It helps if you're raised in the mountains. Two nephews and another boy got lost up there in the Cherokee Forest a couple of winters back. I seen it on TV and I never paid no attention to who it was, and then my sister called. I couldn't understand how they could get lost in there. But then I got to thinking, well, hell—they'd been raised in town. If it had been me, I'd have found me a cave or built me a lean-to . . . you know, take old rotten limbs and prop it up against something and put these leaves on it and move snow around it, and you can survive. I've done that. But they didn't know what to do. They was deer hunting in there and got lost. And the snow came in and they couldn't find their way out. But they finally rescued them.

Last year we went to Tellico, me and Kenny Baker. They wanted to have a little day for me there at this little motel where I go and fish. I saw relatives that I haven't seen in fifty-five years. I didn't know how it would turn out, but we had about two hundred fifty people come up to that camp. And here's Mother[1] and everybody frying fish, and we're trying to feed them all. They wanted to make it an annual thing.

It's just a little dinky place. Mother don't like to go because she has to do the cooking. We go up there and fish. I've got so many friends in those mountains, and they come and say, "Here's nine trout that we caught this morning, and we want you to have them." Then here comes one with ten. . . . They're trying to get rid of them so they can go back and fish again and catch seven at a time, you know, in a period of time.

After we fed all them people up there, I think we had seven rooms in this motel. Me and Mother always gets an apartment. And we cook right out on the water. We brought back twenty-two trout. That was more than we could even handle. They just come and bring them in there. And guys come and they bring their instruments. Everybody just sits around, and they pick all night. Nothing wild—I don't believe in the wild stuff anymore; I won't take Mother around that. We just have a good time. If we want to pick, we will. If you want to drink, that's all right; it don't bother me. There's no law or nothing. I got a second cousin there that runs the place, and he sees that everything is in order, you know . . . if you keep *him* sober.

⇒ Closing Thoughts

If a guy tells you he hasn't had it rough and went without food in this business, he ain't been in there long. I'm not ashamed of it. I'd do it again if I had a shot at it. I might change a few things. The hard times . . . I'd prepare for them. But a musician never does, really. Well, I guess a musician thinks he's going to live forever and going to be young. He doesn't realize the clock runs out on him.

I've been lucky enough in the last twenty years. I don't have to work any more if I don't want to. I see these little old men and little old ladies, their hair is so white and it's beautiful to me. It's a good feeling that you can just kind of call your shots and go where you want to go. I guess you'd call me kind of semiretired. But I made enough in the last twenty, twenty-five years that I'll be all right.

I was in the hospital over there. And when I came to in intensive care my wife was in there. She was holding my hand. And I opened my eyes and there sits Jimmy Martin holding the other hand. My brother was sitting out in the waiting room, and he couldn't get in, but Martin got in there. And he said, "Everything's going to be all right, hoss."

I tell that little thing on stage. I say, "When I woke up, my wife was sitting there . . . she was just a-bawling. She thought I wasn't going to make it, you know. Then I look over there at the other side, and there sat Jimmy Martin holding my other hand and saying, 'Everything's going to be all right.' I didn't know if I'd died and went up yonder or down to the other place, you know." Jimmy Martin got a kick out of that. He said, "Oh, I'm glad you mentioned my name."

I never cared about anything for myself, you know. My family means more to me than anything in this world. The lady I've been married to for forty-seven years has stood by me and supported me in everything I did, and all my children do. We have our discussions, but it's a close-knitted family. I just want to leave something where they could understand the things that I've done that maybe I haven't even told them.

My picking is just an ol' gutsy thing with nothing fancy. It does make me feel pretty good that my efforts were worth it. It makes me feel awfully good that, when I'm gone, I'll leave something that someone can go on with. I'm tickled to death. I've been at it more than fifty years. If my health holds up, I wouldn't mind going another five years or so. But when I quit, I'm gone. I'd just like to go back up in the mountains and stay there.[2]

Testimony from Josh Graves's Contemporaries and Those He Influenced

Josh Graves lived another twelve years after recording the interviews upon which this book is based. In order to convey his remaining story and the lasting impact of his personality and musical innovations, this chapter presents testimonials from twenty-four of Graves's closest associates. These include three generations of his Dobro disciples—many of the best-known living players of that instrument—as well as prominent bandmates from various phases of his career.

The testimonials are organized in roughly the order that their authors encountered Josh Graves. An asterisk (*) indicates that the author's text originally appeared in the unpublished "A Tribute to Josh Graves," compiled by Betty Wheeler and presented to Graves on February 4, 2001. In some of these cases, the editor has shortened the author's copy and modified dated references.

⇒ *Evelyn Graves*

He's been around the world, and I've seen it all through his eyes. I did miss him. The kids were in school. That kept me pretty busy. When he was with Wilma Lee and Stoney, he'd be gone for a week or two, and on Sunday or Monday, when he'd be coming home, it would be like getting ready for a party. I'd get my hair rolled and get the boys cleaned up. I knew he had to be gone. He didn't just belong to me—he belonged to the world.

From "A Day in the Life of Josh Graves," by Marci Shore, Bluegrass Unlimited, *November 2004. Evelyn Hurst Graves met Josh while both were in grade school in East Tennessee. They married when she was fifteen and he, already a traveling musician, was two years older.*

⇒ Earl Scruggs

Josh put the Dobro in bluegrass music. He also took the Dobro far beyond bluegrass. He was extremely versatile and a real trouper. Josh was, and will continue to be, an inspiration to many.

Bluegrass Unlimited *obituary, December 2006. Earl Scruggs (1924-2012) was the world-famous pioneer of the three-finger banjo style. He appeared with Josh Graves in Lester Flatt, Earl Scruggs, and the Foggy Mountain Boys as well as with the Earl Scruggs Revue.*

⇒ Mac Wiseman

To my knowledge, and Josh and I discussed this, I was the first to use the Dobro in a bluegrass band, before he joined Flatt and Scruggs. He'd had a long record with Wilma Lee and Stoney Cooper in Wheeling, West Virginia. I didn't know where he was; I had to track him down. He was working dates with Charlie Bailey in Philadelphia when I hired him. He was going by "Buck" when he was with me. Burkett was his real name.

Josh was with me a couple of years, toward the end of my time in Richmond, Virginia. We could do no wrong with records, and there weren't enough days in the year . . . we'd work three hundred one-nighters. I hired him mainly to play the Dobro. I've always done a lot of ballads and sentimental songs, and I felt like the banjo was too harsh for that material. He'd fill in with mandolin on the up-tempo tunes. I was a big fan of the blues as well. We had many wonderful sessions in the dressing room with just "low-down" blues. I always told him he was part black, because he'd play those old Lightnin' Hopkins things.

Josh, as Oswald[1] would say, "put a lot of honey in it." He played colorful things that fit the material. I felt so secure when he was playing background with me, because he knew exactly what to do. I had a little philosophy with every band member, "You don't have to be as good as Chet Atkins, but I want all you've got. When I'm singing, I want you to make me sound as good as you can. And when I'm featuring you on an instrumental, I'll do everything I can to put you over to the audience."

Josh was one of the best fellows that ever worked for me. He was very cooperative. If anything, he would cause a little dissension in the band by being too willing to help; they felt like he was playing up to the boss to get more attention. At that time Josh couldn't drive, but he rode shotgun better than anybody in the world, avoiding accidents. Several times he woke me up when I was driving. His trailer was parked behind mine in a trailer park on north Highway 1 out of Richmond, so we saw his family a lot. His kids were real small, and Evelyn took care of Carol Lee Cooper as well, when Wilma Lee and Stoney were on the road.

Josh and I stayed in close touch after he went with Flatt and Scruggs. He was on numerous recordings with me in the later years. After I disbanded and was working solo dates, if Josh was there, he'd come out and work with me because he enjoyed playing those old songs. The last date we did was up at J. D. Crowe's festival. His wife, Evelyn, was with him, and we had a long talk backstage. He went out and did his bit, and when I came on, he stayed and played with me, J. D. Crowe, and Bobby Osborne. That was history there! He and I had planned to participate in the late show with the IBMA[2] the day he died. We kept calling back and forth saying, "I'll do it if you'll do it."

He deserved a lot more credit than he got. He was very inventive. He would listen to the earlier Dobro players, but he wasn't a copier of anybody. He'd put his own turn on it and was very conscientious to complement the songs you were singing. That's what I liked about him so much.

Mac Wiseman, a member of the Bluegrass Hall of Fame, has been a headlining star in bluegrass and country music since the early 1950s, following sideman stints with Molly O'Day, Bill Monroe, and Flatt and Scruggs. A Virginian, he is known as "The Voice with a Heart."

➣ *George "Speedy" Krise*

Josh and I were friends for more than fifty-five years. Now, that is not that we ran around or chummed around together. Because we lived in different places, our paths crossed only once in a while, usually at a music festival or program of some kind. But when we did get together, we enjoyed our friendship very much.

I had left Knoxville and was playing on the radio at Oak Hill, West Virginia. I had gotten my friend Mac Wiseman to play a number of show dates at different towns around that area. Mac and his band stayed at my house until it was time to perform. Josh was in Mac's band, and he was playing mandolin at the time. Go figure!

One time when I was visiting Nashville for several weeks, Lester Flatt heard I was in town and sent a car around to the hotel to take me out to the radio station where the Foggy Mountain Boys were making some transcriptions. When I walked through the door, Josh saw me and was all smiles. That proved to be a great friendship day for us all.

Another time, after I had moved to Ohio, Josh came to play at a community event, and I went out to see and be with him that night. We did some Dobro playing onstage together. I think one of the numbers we did was "I'll Be All Smiles Tonight." Josh had a wry sense of humor. He told the audience, "I always look forward to coming here in the worst way." Of course they laughed, knowing he was kidding about the town. I played with Josh onstage at a few other sites, including Union Town, Ohio. Kenny Baker was with him on that one.

Through the years we talked about making an album together, but somehow we never got around to getting that accomplished.

The last time I saw Josh was at the Tennessee Homecoming Festival in Norris, Tennessee. My daughter took a picture of Kenny Baker, John Hartford, Josh, and me together. I framed it, and it's now on my wall, a prized possession. After that, the tragic health problems fell upon Josh. It was all so very, very sad. But he kept in good spirits and just went on being himself. That was the kind of man he was, God bless him.

Josh was a great person. I'm proud and honored that he was a good friend. He was my all-out, overall favorite Dobro player. I loved him.

George "Speedy" Krise (1922–2011), a West Virginian, was one of the Dobro pioneers in country music, cited by Josh Graves as one of his early influences. In the late 1940s and early 1950s, Krise toured and recorded with Molly O'Day and Carl Butler and wrote well-known songs, including "Going Like Wildfire" and "Georgia Waltz."

⇒ *Lance LeRoy*

Burkett Graves will always be "Uncle Josh" to me and millions of other people. I don't think a better showman and musician ever existed. Like many others, I became a fan of Josh in 1955 when he began with Lester and Earl. Over the years we became close friends, and I was privileged to travel many miles with him on Lester's bus when the two of us worked for Lester Flatt.

Josh was a devoted husband, father, grandfather, and great-grandfather. His widow, Evelyn, is one of the finest people I've known. I miss Josh greatly and think of him often.

Lance LeRoy, a member of the Bluegrass Hall of Fame, is a Nashville-based booking agent and a founder of the International Bluegrass Music Association. He was Lester Flatt's personal manager from 1969 until Flatt's death in 1979.

≫ Robert "Tut" Taylor

Burkett H. Graves—Buck Graves—Uncle Josh—call him by any name and he responded, usually with a big grin. He was always kind and gracious, especially to those with a head full of questions. Josh was a hero to many and a true showman. He was my friend.

Josh was always busy onstage and kept things lively. He brought a wonderful sound with his new style of Dobro playing. They were astounded at his ability to play a roll like he did; it was almost like when Earl Scruggs introduced the three-finger banjo roll on the *Grand Ole Opry*. The band was very tight, and their ability to weave in and out of position to take their breaks was a sight to behold. Of all the group, I think Josh was the master of this choreography.

There was a side to him not mentioned by many. I was fortunate to attend a lot of the Foggy Mountain Boys' shows, and it was always a pleasure to watch Josh play his part as a comedian, usually with Cousin Jake, Kentucky Slim, and others in the band. This was an essential part of the show; comedy was very important in the early days. Not only was it a crowd-pleaser, but it gave Lester and Earl a little breathing time backstage. Most of the time, Josh was dressed in some outlandish outfit. He also sang a lot, with Cousin Jake taking the high tenor part. Josh and Jake were always a hit with the audiences; they were almost a show of their own. I'm sorry this part of performing tradition became lost over the years.

As the years slowly passed, the sounds of the Dobro in Josh's hands appealed to many, and more players appeared on the scene. New styles and techniques evolved. The Dobro found a home in bluegrass. It has been stated by many that Bill Monroe didn't like the Dobro, but you can't like the blues and not like the Dobro. Bill did not want to sound like Roy Acuff, so he never added a Dobro to his own group.

The sound of the Dobro has permeated this big globe we live on. I give Josh credit for this. There are some that have copied his style, but not the soul he put into it. That belonged to him and him alone.

Robert "Tut" Taylor, originally of Milledgeville, Georgia, was one of the earliest followers of bluegrass music. His unique style of Dobro playing, using a flat pick, was heard on many recordings beginning in the 1960s, including John Hartford's Dobrolic Plectral Society (Aereo-Plane Band). Taylor coproduced Grammy Award-winner The Great Dobro Sessions, *a multiartist project, in 1994.*

⇒ LeRoy Mack (McNees)*

As I sit down to write a few thoughts, so many memories fill my mind. I remember the first time I heard Josh Graves play. I wasn't even into bluegrass music at the time. A friend of mine was all excited about a new album he had just bought and wanted to play it for me. So we sat down in his living room, and he put it on the turntable. Little did I know that the next three minutes would change the rest of my life. He played "Randy Lynn Rag," and I was hooked. It took a while to figure out what those instruments were and how they were played, but that sound . . . wow! I heard some live bluegrass on the radio and went right down to the place where they were playing. That is where I met Roland and Clarence White. I hung out with them for a while until Roland said, "Why don't you get a Dobro and join the band?" That is when I started to learn how to play the Dobro.

I sat up many hours with Josh on the record player at half speed, picking out each note and slide. Then came the day in 1959 when Roland and I drove to Nashville to see Flatt and Scruggs. Josh was so gracious to us. We followed the bus around each night to the little schoolhouses to see him play. It was like magic to see and hear the music at the same time, because I had only heard it on record before. I went home inspired to keep on learning the Dobro. I never would have believed it then if someone told me that someday Josh and I would write songs together and that he would play on my recording. But it happened.

For the last fifty years, I have been playing the Dobro, and I guess I should be a whole lot better at it than I am by now. But it has been an absolute blessing in so many ways. First of all, I met my wife, Jan, when playing at the Ash Grove. I have met countless people, traveled countless miles, and touched countless lives with the music that Josh passed on to me. My goal is to pass it on in turn to as many people as I can.

LeRoy Mack (McNees), a native of Los Angeles, toured, recorded, and appeared on the Andy Griffith Show *with the Country Boys, later to become the Kentucky Colonels, in the early 1960s. He has continued to record and perform on the Dobro as a sideline to his business career.*

⇒ *Russ Hooper*

In 1951 I became aware of Buck. He was playing with Wilma Lee and Stoney Cooper. I followed his music after that and eventually developed a long friendship with him. Buck was a source of great encouragement and was my IDOL! I listened to his music and learned a great deal from him. No matter how much we strive to play like him, there will never be another Buck Graves.

I don't know anybody who was NOT influenced by him in one way or another!

Russ Hooper, from the Baltimore area, was one of the earliest disciples of Josh Graves. Beginning in the early 1960s, he recorded on Dobro with Jim Eanes and several of the early Baltimore-Washington bands.

⇒ *Bobby Wolfe**

What can one say about Uncle Josh—Buck Graves—Burkett Graves—that hasn't already been said many times? Probably the best personal compliment I can pay is: "Josh was always Josh every time you saw him." There aren't many people you can say that about after knowing them for more than thirty-five years.

I have many stories from him and about him, but my favorite is from a visit to his home in the '60s. It had been a long day, it was suppertime, and we had planned to go to a local restaurant. However, we had popped a few tops, and Josh suggested we cook a fish he had. While cooking, we continued to talk, and I happened to mention one of my favorite songs, Wilma Lee and Stoney Cooper's recording of "Come Walk with Me." Josh said, "Thank you" and showed me his BMI award for the song. I was speechless. This was my introduction to Josh the songwriter.

Not only is Josh the father of bluegrass Dobro, but he is also a great songwriter. The latest count of recordings I remember is around one hundred fifty. "Come Walk with Me" was probably one of the first big ones for him commercially and financially. Look around and you'll be surprised at the songs with the Graves name on them. I haven't heard a bad one yet: "Fireball" . . . "Just Joshing" . . . "Shuckin' the Corn" . . . "Someone You Have Forgotten" . . . "If You're Ever Going to Love Me" . . . "Evelina" . . . "Flatt Lonesome" . . . "The Good Things Outweigh the Bad" . . . "Ten Miles from Natchez" . . . "Foggy Mountain Rock" . . . and on and on. Let's hear it for Josh the songwriter!

Bobby Wolfe, proprietor of Wolfe Resonator Guitars, Davidson, North Carolina, is renowned for his new instruments, restorations, knowledge, and enthusiasm for "all things resonator."

ᐳ Mike Auldridge*

Josh Graves basically defined what I was going to do with my life when I was fourteen years old. He zapped me several more times in my late teens and then in my twenties, but that first encounter was what sealed my fate.

I had been exposed to the Dobro guitar by my uncle Ellsworth Cozzens when I was a small child. Ellsworth had played steel on Jimmie Rodgers's recordings in 1928 and was the family hero. I loved to watch him play at family gatherings and thought it was a cool sound, but it wasn't until I heard Josh playing on the radio with Wilma Lee and Stoney Cooper when I was fourteen that I was totally hooked on "that sound."

Josh played very differently from my uncle. Josh played with such *fire and passion*. His playing was so new to my ears that I didn't even realize that he was playing the same instrument. On the radio, Stoney Cooper called it an "old-time steel." I pictured it as some ornate-looking thing with legs that probably had feet on it, like an old-time bathtub. In fact, I used to draw pictures in school of what I imagined it looked like. I was fascinated with the sound of something that I wasn't even sure existed.

I listened every Saturday night to their show on the *Old Dominion Barn Dance* from Richmond, Virginia. Finally, after months of listening, I had the opportunity to actually go to the *Barn Dance*, which was not a dance at all, but a radio program held in a big, beautiful theater in downtown Richmond. Our car broke down on the way, and we ended up arriving at the theater after Wilma Lee and Stoney's set was finished. I was really bummed. We watched Mac Wiseman, who was another of my favorites, close the show and then had the unbelievable good fortune of being invited to the radio studio in a hotel that was next door to the auditorium, where both bands played a live midnight show.

The radio station man led us to a row of six or seven chairs that were set up along the wall of the small studio where the "after-hours" midnight show was about to begin. We were the only audience! The band walked in the room, and I could hardly believe my eyes. . . . There was Buck Graves (as he was then known) in person! And he was holding a guitar like the one my uncle played! Was that what they were calling an "old-time steel," I wondered? That can't be! When they broke into their first song, "Stoney, Are You Mad at Your Girl?" (which was pretty much the same song as "Ruby," which the Osborne Brothers recorded years later), and Josh burned the strings off that guitar with a fast and furious rolling break, I could hardly contain my glee. Every note he played that night went right to my soul. Even the slow stuff killed me. I was really hooked now.

I had been a huge fan of Flatt and Scruggs for several years and loved that style of "hillbilly" music. There was no distinction, at that time, between what have become known as bluegrass and country. I loved it all. Most of my favorite bands had a Dobro: Johnnie and Jack, Molly O'Day, Mac O'Dell, and, of course, Wilma Lee and Stoney Cooper. When Josh Graves left the Coopers and joined Flatt and Scruggs in 1955, that was my idea of a perfect band.

My brother and I and a couple of our school buddies had a band by this time. I always wanted to be the banjo player, but my friend Wayne Mason was much better than I was, so I played guitar. My brother also played guitar, but two guitars in a band just wasn't how it was done. When Josh Graves joined Flatt and Scruggs, that was the defining moment that changed everything. Now it was OK to have a Dobro in a bluegrass-style band. That was all I needed. I started looking for a Dobro guitar, which was very hard to find in those days. I soon found one and started copying every note that Josh played on those Flatt and Scruggs records.

Years later, after I had spent two years in the Army and was going to the University of Maryland, I was teaching guitar, banjo, and Dobro in a music store as a part-time job. One of my students, a woman named Betty Jones, and her husband, Grady Jones, became friends with Josh and used to invite him to stay with them whenever he was passing through with Flatt and Scruggs. They invited me over one day to meet him and Johnny Johnson, who was also working in the Flatt and Scruggs band.

Josh and Johnny were sitting around the kitchen table playing, and they insisted that I play something for them. I'll never forget the feeling I got when Josh said, "Man, you play smooth . . . that was great." That was the next time Josh sealed my fate. To get an encouraging word from my hero made me decide that if I ever had half a chance, I would become a musician. I cut classes for the rest of the week and played the tapes that Grady made of them playing, over and over again. I studied every lick on that tape and probably spent more hours trying to be a good Dobro player than I did at trying to be a good student.

A few years later, I was fortunate enough to be in the right place at the right time and ended up helping form the Seldom Scene. Nothing that I've done musically with my life would have happened without Josh Graves inspiring me over and over again through the years. He is still my hero.

Mike Auldridge, a Washington, DC, native, came to prominence in the 1970s with Emerson and Waldron and as a founding member of the Seldom Scene. Auldridge is also known for an influential series of solo albums.

☙ Curtis Burch

The first time I ever heard a Dobro was on the radio, in about 1956. It was Uncle Josh Graves playing "Foggy Mountain Rock." I did not know who was playing it or what the instrument was, but I was forever captivated by the sound. My dad had been teaching me acoustic guitar, and I had been playing for about a year. Dad said he would find out about the sound we heard. I think he called the DJ, who told him who the band was and the name of the instrument.

It turned out that a friend of ours from down the street had a couple of Flatt and Scruggs LPs. I would go there every day after school, listen to them, and try to figure out how to play the tunes when I got back to my house. Soon I had my own turntable, bought all the Flatt and Scruggs records I could find, and learned everything Josh did.

Around 1962, Flatt and Scruggs were to perform at the coliseum in nearby Jacksonville, Florida, along with many other *Opry* performers. When we got there, I told my dad to go in and get his seat. I was going to try to get backstage to meet Josh. I met Jim McReynolds at the back door. He remembered me from recent performances in my hometown of Brunswick, Georgia, where they were gracious enough to have me as a guest. I found Josh backstage, walked right up to him, and introduced myself. He treated me like a long-lost friend. I was on top of the world meeting and talking to my hero. That day I was inspired by his humility as well as his musicianship.

I didn't see Josh again until I moved to Nashville, many years later. By and by, I got to play some gigs with him on guitar. For a long time, I didn't dare play Dobro in front of him. Then, in 1993, we did the *Great Dobro Sessions* album, produced by Jerry Douglas and Tut Taylor, and it won a Grammy! It was an honor to record with my hero Uncle Josh Graves. After that, I would talk with him on the phone every now and then. A few years later, we played at the SPBGMA in his honor. That was the last time I saw him.

I'll never forget the man that started bluegrass Dobro playing and who inspired me with his performance of "Foggy Mountain Rock." But even more so, I remember Josh as a human being who had time for his friends and fans and never felt or acted like he was above anyone. I thank Uncle Josh Graves for introducing me to an instrument that has taken me on a journey through life. On that journey, I have met many other people that share the love and camaraderie that bluegrass generates—like no other kind of music—and that continues to this day.

Curtis Burch, who grew up in Alabama and Georgia, now lives in Kentucky. A founding member of the New Grass Revival, he is currently an instructor in the bluegrass program at Hazard Community and Technical College.

➢ *Herb Pedersen**

It was the summer of 1967. I moved to Nashville from Berkeley, California. I heard Josh play live for the first time backstage at the Ryman Auditorium. I realized two things right then. Josh did for the Dobro what Earl Scruggs had done for the five-string banjo, and my musical life, whatever that was going to be, would always be influenced by these two men.

If there is a defining moment in the development of the Dobro, for me it is Josh's solo on "Home Sweet Home" on the *Foggy Mountain Banjo* album. It's as real as it gets. Josh has always been a great help to young players, and I'm no exception. As rare as it was that I got to see him, a day doesn't go by when I don't think about the wonderful music he was a big part in developing.

God bless you, Uncle . . .

Herb Pedersen, from the San Francisco area, is now based near Los Angeles. Renowned for his banjo playing and tenor voice, he has played and recorded with many leading acts in bluegrass and country music, including Emmylou Harris and the Hot Band, the Desert Rose Band, the Laurel Canyon Rangers, and a brief stint with the Foggy Mountain Boys while Earl Scruggs was recovering from an operation.

≫ Ron Mesing*

My earliest recollection of the Dobro was in the late '50s and early '60s, watching a couple of Dobro players named Shot Jackson and Bashful Brother Oswald at the WWVA Jamboree in Wheeling, West Virginia. They both had a smooth, sweet, pleasant sound that adhered strictly to the melody.

One day my dad gave me a Flatt and Scruggs record. Some of the cuts on it were "Randy Lynn Rag," "Shuckin' the Corn," and "Foggy Mountain Special." This album blew me away. I loved everything about it. Although I was a banjo player at the time and thrilled to hear Earl's pickin', there was another instrument on the album that had a different sound I did not recognize but that definitely caught my ear. It was a driving, swooping, sliding, crying, and moaning bluesy "bucket" sound. I thought it was some type of a modified guitar. I didn't know that a Dobro could be played like that! From that day on, I was a loyal Flatt and Scruggs/Josh Graves fan.

I first met Josh when he was with the Earl Scruggs Revue. I had an old Flatt and Scruggs album called *Bonnie and Clyde* that had some great blues licks on it that Josh had done, especially on a cut called "Getaway." I could not pick up all of the licks because of the siren and squealing-tire sound effects mixed over his break. When I met Josh, I asked him if he could show me some of the blues licks that were on that album. To my surprise, he told me he could not remember exactly what he had played. What a letdown! Although he was very polite to me, I thought that he really did not want to show me the licks.

Instruction videos and other types of teaching aids were not available at that time. The only way you learned was from other Dobro players' records. Most of them would keep trade secrets close to the vest and not show their best licks. I went home frustrated and determined that I was going to master Josh's style. I practiced six to eight hours a day, working on the Graves technique.

One day a young Dobro player came up to me after a set and asked me to show him a lick that I did on a record many years ago. To my surprise I didn't even remember recording the song, let alone the lick that I used. Then it hit me, a flashback from ten years ago: When I asked Josh for a lick and he didn't remember, he really was being honest with me!

Over the years my wife, Debbie, and I became good friends with Josh and his family. We have many fond memories of Josh. I have been fortunate enough not only to meet my childhood idol but also to record with him on an album called *The Graves Digger*. We named our firstborn son Josh as a tribute to "Uncle."

Even though other Dobro players may take the instrument to new heights, the Graves style will continue to be the foundation for the Dobro, just as the Scruggs style is the foundation for the banjo.

Ron Mesing, of Finleyville, Pennsylvania, has recorded two solo Dobro albums. He came to prominence with Red Allen and the Kentuckians during the 1970s.

≫ Jerry Douglas*

On a summer evening in Ottawa, Ohio, a twelve-year-old boy waited to meet his idol. It was said that Josh Graves would be over at his friends' camp to play a little bit before going on Lester Flatt's bus to the next show date somewhere. While the other kids chased each other through the park, the boy waited and wondered what Josh would be like. Would he just smile and say, "That's nice, kid. Now go away and play with your friends," or would he even show up? The boy had been practicing "Fireball" and "Maggie Blues" all day.

After almost giving up, there was a rise from the small crowd around the campfire and into the light walked Paul Warren and Uncle Josh with their cases. Around the fire, the band stopped playing and welcomed their esteemed guests. Maybe somebody passed around a bottle, then Josh pulled the Holy Grail of Dobros out of its case. The boy's eyes became as big as saucers as he approached the man whom he had heard on records or on the radio each morning before school for the last three years.

The boy walked up to the fire with his shiny new Dobro as Josh leaned over to his friend saying, "Is this the kid you were talking about?" His friend answered, "Yes," as Josh took off his strap. Handing the Grail to me, he said, "Here, kid. You play this old box and let me try yours." I'll never forget, the neck of that guitar was so scratched and used that it felt like a piece of driftwood in my hands. As soon as I got my breath again, we played "Fireball" and then "Just Joshin.'" We jammed late into the night. I was at ease with the way he had treated me . . . the kid who tried to copy every note Josh played.

I will remain forever grateful for the lessons I received that night. Josh not only inspired me to be a better musician, but also to give any young musician the time and attention that he or she deserves.

Jerry Douglas, a native of Warren, Ohio, became a prominent Dobro player in bluegrass music through his appearances and recordings with the Country Gentlemen, J. D. Crowe and the New South, and Boone Creek in the 1970s. Between 1990 and 2009, he was voted the Dobro Player of the Year eight times by the International Bluegrass Music Association. He is a featured member of Alison Krauss and Union Station and records widely in a variety of genres.

⇒ *Stacy Phillips**

Buck was the first player I ever saw play Dobro. After the concert I asked him if he had any extra guitars. When the bus pulled out a half hour later, I was standing on a New York City street corner with a National metal body and Buck's steel bar in my hands.

The only technique I really tried to copy was the way Buck swooped in and away when taking a solo, tilting the instrument up to the mic and standing on tiptoe. At the Bean Blossom festival when Flatt and Monroe finally sang together after decades—when Bill sang lead, Buck dug in and played some busy, belligerent backup.

I would not be playing a Dobro professionally if it weren't for Buck Graves. And the few times I had a chance to informally chat with him— what great stories he had to tell.

My favorite Buck Graves cuts from the Flatt and Scruggs days include "False Hearted Lover," "A Hundred Years from Now," "On My Mind," "Shuckin' the Corn," "Dobro Rhumba," "Reuben," "Confessin'," and, of course, "Salty Dog Blues."

Stacy Phillips, a resonator guitarist and violin player, has three solo albums, performed with Breakfast Special and Tasty Licks, and is heard on the Grammy Award-winning album The Great Dobro Sessions. *He is the author of more than twenty-five books and DVDs on various aspects of his chosen instruments.*

⇒ Tim Graves*

Uncle Josh and I were more like father and son than uncle and nephew. He brought me my first Dobro when I was fifteen years old. He told me that if I would learn to play it that it would always take care of me. This has proved true many times already. I want to say thank you, Uncle Josh, for paving the way for me and all other Dobro players. If it had not been for him, the Dobro would not be where it is today. I consider it an honor to walk in his footsteps, and I will always do my best to uphold the standards that he set for all of us in the music and in the professionalism.

Tim Graves, from Tellico Plains, Tennessee, is the son of Josh Graves's brother Dick. He has backed well-known Nashville artists, played with Bobby Osborne and the Rocky Top X-Press, and headed his own band, Cherokee.

⇒ Sally Van Meter*

I first met Josh at the 1976 Grass Valley Bluegrass Festival. I remember watching him and just falling in love with his playing. I got up the courage to go up and introduce myself, and he was immediately encouraging. He handed me his Dobro right away, and the first thing that happened was that his strap came off the end pin, and away to the ground went his guitar! Being the kind soul and gentleman that he was, he never showed any annoyance toward me about that incident.

Talk about being nervous and feeling just a bit more than clumsy! He didn't react negatively, instead just asked me if I wanted to sit down and play a bit, and he then proceeded to hand me a lifetime's worth of inspiration. For about the next hour or two, he sat down with me and taught me how to play the tune "Fireball." He granted me great patience, as I was still in the beginning stages of playing slide guitar. After having this one experience, I went out and bought quite a few Flatt and Scruggs recordings, just for his playing. What I got out of that little session was a lasting impression of what great tone and strong playing are all about and, importantly, inspiration—serious inspiration.

What does Josh mean to me? He was a friend and a player I was fortunate to spend musical time with, for which I will forever be thankful. He is a major contributor to my reasons for playing resonator guitar. I listened to him as a small child, my parents being big bluegrass fans. There was a great sound that he offered up in Flatt and Scruggs, something quite different from Bill Monroe's bluegrass sound. He was the Dobro player that was always able to stand right up there with Earl Scruggs and find a way to play all those fast songs and instrumentals and have it work perfectly with the banjo rolls that ruled Flatt and Scruggs's sound. Add into that Josh's own inimitable style, with such strong tone and bluesy, melodic ideas. Who could ask for more? The first tune that I remember hearing him play was "Home Sweet Home." What a sound, what a feel—traditional and sweet, but with a fast, mean hint of the blues in his playing. I was fascinated. When you listen to Josh, you know it is JOSH. I just love that.

So many players I work with tell me that Josh is their main reason for picking up the Dobro. We all love his playing for its bluesy feel and hot licks, and I am certain that we have all (gratefully) absconded with a solid collection of Josh licks and solos. When I teach resonator guitar classes, I always try to include a classic Josh solo. To me, all reso players owe him so much for his many years of breaking trail for us.

Sally Van Meter, originally from the San Francisco Bay area, now lives in Colorado. One of the top Dobro players in bluegrass since her work with the Good Ol' Persons from 1977 to 1996, she has won awards for her playing and has toured and recorded with such musical greats as Chris Hillman, Peter Rowan, Jerry Garcia, and Jorma Kaukonen and has worn the producer's hat for the Yonder Mountain String Band, Open Road, and others.

⇒ Rob Ickes*

When I started playing, one of the first bluegrass albums my brother and I had was *Foggy Mountain Banjo*. It was absolutely incredible! Josh's playing fit so perfectly with what Flatt and Scruggs were doing. And that has been inspiring to me: a great combination of people playing together, playing what fits the song, and doing material that fits that combination of people. That's what I aspire to with my band, Blue Highway.

Josh was the right man at the right time. It's not like the guitar, where there are a million players. On the Dobro, there are just a handful of players who have done groundbreaking work. Josh is one of those few; he is one of the most important people, if not *the* most important person on the instrument. One of the many things I learned from Josh was his feel for the blues, which is something that fits the instrument perfectly. He understood that and made it work, and he broke a lot of ground in that respect. It was a huge change to what had been thought possible on the instrument, similar to how Earl Scruggs changed what people thought was possible on the banjo.

One of the other things I appreciated about Josh was his sense of humor. He had that until the very end. Ronnie McCoury told me a story recently. Terry Eldridge went to visit Josh in the hospital after his second leg amputation. Josh was lying there with the tubes in him and all the machines hooked up. He motioned for Terry to come closer so he could tell him something important. When Terry knelt down, Josh said, "Can you lend me $50 'til I get back on my feet?" I think it takes a lot of spirit to joke around at a time like that. Josh had that spirit in spades!

You could never put in words the importance of his playing to the development of the instrument. Josh is truly an inspiration to me. He always has been and always will be.

Rob Ickes has been voted Dobro Player of the Year by the International Bluegrass Music Association twelve times between 1990 and 2010. A founding member of Blue Highway and Three Ring Circle, he also regularly performs with his jazz ensemble and is the founder of ResoSummit, a three-day educational event held in Nashville each year.

≫ Fred Travers*

I had the great fortune of meeting Josh Graves nearly two decades ago at the Bass Mountain Bluegrass Festival in North Carolina. I was playing Dobro with Paul Adkins and the Borderline band at the time and was quite overwhelmed to be performing on the same stage with this legendary figure.

I gathered enough courage to walk up and introduce myself along with his many other fans. He was gracious and patient as I nervously made conversation. He was very generous with his knowledge and experiences as I asked what seemed to be dozens of questions about his playing style and influences. I will always be very grateful for that.

I would like to personally thank Josh Graves for sharing his talents and music with us and for his enormous contributions to country and bluegrass music. I also thank him for establishing a place for the Dobro guitar in bluegrass music and a standard of excellence that we, as players, humbly try to measure up to with each performance.

Fred Travers, from Huntingtown, Maryland, learned to play Dobro from Mike Auldridge and took over his chair on that instrument when Auldridge left the Seldom Scene in 1995.

≫ Betty Wheeler*

I didn't hear much bluegrass music until I was firmly middle-aged, and I started learning to play the resonator guitar in late 1999, having seen it played just a few times. At one of my first lessons, my teacher, Michael Witcher, asked me what reso players I was listening to. I mentioned Jerry Douglas, Rob Ickes, and *The Great Dobro Sessions*. Michael gave me the sternest look a nineteen-year-old can muster and said, "You must listen to Flatt and Scruggs. That's the foundation for all Dobro playing." In my woeful ignorance, after my lesson I asked someone about "Scruggs and Flatt," then wondered why an aspiring reso player should listen to a banjo player or guitarist. But I soon realized that he was ordering me to listen to Josh Graves.

Since that time, I've listened as carefully as I can to every Josh recording I can find, from all periods of his career. I listen to the great players talk about his contributions and influence, but an even more telling tribute is to listen for that influence in their music—in the best players, it's always there, woven seamlessly into their own styles of playing, but still identifiably "Josh." The more I hear and learn, the more I have come to understand how revolutionary and enduring are the contributions he has made to resonator guitar playing and to music—bluegrass and beyond. I've certainly learned enough to know that as an aspiring reso player, I will be studying at Josh Graves University for many years to come.

In the course of editing the tribute book the Dobro community presented to Josh at the SPGBMA[3] in 2001, I learned something even more inspiring: the generosity with which Josh Graves shared his expertise, his time, his patience, and his wonderful heart and zest for life—seemingly with everyone who ever crossed his path. It isn't possible to capture all the great stories that are out there about Josh, but it was a lot of fun to try.

Betty Wheeler coproduces ResoSummit with Rob Ickes. A San Diego-based attorney, she organized and edited A Tribute to Josh Graves *in 2001.*

⤜ *Eddie and Martha Adcock*

Josh Graves is an honest-to-goodness hero of bluegrass music. Aside from his tremendous creativity and technical musicianship, what we love about his playing is that he was, unquestionably, the king of tone . . . it was fabulously deep and rich, as soulful and expressive as a human voice.

Eddie says, "Josh and I go 'way back to before they invented dirt. Everybody loved Josh's playing, for sure, and even the most casual listener was attracted to it; but back in the days when he would come hang out around the Washington, DC, scene with us to visit and jam, I've heard him play stuff that would just scare the pants off you, it was so far above most everybody's head."

Uncle Josh loved all kinds of music, but he especially had a great appreciation for and a huge, deep knowledge of the blues. Blues music fueled him as much as any kind ever did, and that is evident in his playing. If we went over to his house, even before his sweet wife, Evelyn, could offer a cup of coffee, Uncle Josh would say, "Come over here. I want you to listen to something," and it would be a recording of some ancient, obscure blues dude from the cotton fields of Louisiana or Mississippi. It would be something that was very fine and funky, and he wanted to share it because he knew we'd like it, too. We still have several cassette tapes he made for us. He never stopped being excited about music.

Besides being one of a kind, Uncle Josh was a jewel of a guy and a really sweet friend. Of course, he had an edge, too, or he wouldn't have survived in the business all those years. And he was funny—so funny!—full of wisecracks and stories. He had more road stories than anyone we've ever known and a readiness to relate them to an appreciative audience. Some were for musicians' ears only . . . some of them would have to wait for publication until all the protagonists had died!

Eddie fronted the Masters "super group" of the late '80s and '90s. Says Martha, "Josh, along with Kenny Baker and Jesse McReynolds—all icons in our music—accepted Missy Raines and me as peers instead of just a female rhythm section. Every day, they made us feel validated as fellow musicians and troupers. In the blink of an eye, those guys became my dear friends. Always, when Josh would spot me at a show or a festival, he would grin, look me up and down, and then put his hand over his heart and say, 'Help me, Elizabeth, I think I'm gonna have the big one!'[4] I never, ever saw Josh in a bad mood."

Despite multiple hospitalizations for numerous ailments, Josh kept a wonderful attitude. Even when he had a leg amputated, and then the other, he stayed cheerful. If you asked how he was doing, he'd say, "Well, I can't kick . . ."

Here's a little story his wife, Evelyn, told us. In the hospital room beside Josh was a young man who'd had a leg amputated and was extremely depressed. When he found out that Josh was his roommate, he could scarcely believe it, because his favorite musical heroes were Flatt and Scruggs as well as Reno and Smiley. Well, here was Josh cheering up this kid who'd lost his leg below the knee, when Josh himself now had both of his legs gone. Josh called Don Wayne and Dale Reno to come over, and he arranged with the nurses to find them an empty room. Josh and Don Wayne and Dale all played some music for this kid! Evelyn said it was great therapy for *all* of them.

Josh requested Eddie to build him a pickin' table to put his Dobro on. "I don't have a lap anymore," he pointed out, "and I've got a show to play in Mississippi." Eddie asked him when he was scheduled to leave, and Josh said, "Tomorrow." So Eddie got busy, went and measured everything, and built him a little folding table overnight. Martha added a little piece of rug padding he could throw on top, so the Dobro wouldn't slide around.

He meant so much to us. We still pinch ourselves that we were able to call this musical giant a friend and that he felt the same way about us. It's hard to tell you how grateful and honored we feel to have gotten the chance to get to know "Uncle" so well. It was enlightening, too, we can tell you that!

Thank goodness his nephew Tim Graves tours the bluegrass circuit nowadays. Tim's Dobro sound and style comes closer to Josh's than anyone else's does, or could.

Banjo pioneer Eddie Adcock, a Virginia native and member of the classic Country Gentlemen, also toured with Mac Wiseman, Bill Monroe, the II Generation, and the Masters. Former South Carolinian guitarist and vocalist Martha Hearon married Eddie in 1976. The couple currently work as a duo.

⇒ Phil Leadbetter

It was Josh Graves who made me want to play the Dobro! I don't think anyone that plays the three-finger style would have played that way if it hadn't been for him. There would have been the Dobro, but it wouldn't have sounded the way we hear it in bluegrass now.

The style that Josh brought in was just so "ear catching." My brother was a banjo player, and I remember him bringing the Flatt and Scruggs records home. My brother enjoyed what Earl was playing, but it was that other instrument that I kept hearing in there that I really liked. I asked my brother, "What is that?" and he told me it was a Dobro. It was right then that I wanted to play one. I had to play.

I started playing in November of 1974. I was twelve and had been playing about three months when I heard that Josh was going to be at the Capitol Theatre, right across the street from my friend Roy Garrett's record store in Maryville, Tennessee. As we started closing in on the week for that, I kept getting more and more nervous. Josh Graves was going to be there! I skipped the last two days of school before the show, laying out to practice up on some of my Josh stuff. I brought my Dobro with me that night. I just wanted to have him sign it if I was brave enough to ask him.

They told me, "Josh just came in the back door." I ran to the bathroom real quick to make sure that my shirt was tucked in and my hair was right (I had hair back then). Well, I popped in and hit Josh with the door. I normally would have run, but after I almost killed him with the door, I shook hands and told him I played Dobro.

Later on that night, he asked if I wanted to get up on the stage and play a song with him. He said, "My nephew's going to play." That's the first time I met Tim Graves. Josh asked what I wanted to play, and "Shuckin' the Corn" was the only tune I knew real good off that album with the big rainbow on it. He looked over at me to take a break and I thought, "I don't think I can play in front of you," but I did!

Josh had things a little different; he was real unconventional. Where most people would say, "Oh, this is close, this is easy to get right here," Josh would throw you a curve. He would hit it from a different place on the neck. You might have the right note, but it would never sound exactly his way. Josh was a "sneaky" player. He played things that were tricky to get. A lot of people emulate the sound he got, but nobody will ever sound just like him.

In 2001, some of us talked Chuck Stearman into doing something for Josh at the SPBGMA, because Josh had been overlooked on a lot of awards. We used Resoguit-L, the resonator guitar list on the Internet, to organize the tribute and raise funds for a special plaque to present to him.

We invited Dobro players, both professional and amateur, to participate in the special tribute. Many of the best-known players were onstage for the tribute, including Jerry Douglas, Mike Auldridge, Randy Kohrs, Rob Ickes, Tim Graves, Gene Wooten, Curtis Burch, and LeRoy Mack. Behind them, the stage was filled with more than forty additional players. We played "Fireball"—which Josh wrote—presented a plaque and tribute album to him, and then Josh played one of his classic tunes, "Flatt Lonesome." It meant a lot to him to have so many people onstage who were influenced by him.

Josh told me one time when he had his first leg taken off, "The doctors told me it was going to cost me an arm and a leg . . . I'm half way there." Josh would joke about things like that. He wasn't a guy that sat down and said, "I can't do this anymore." I remember Josh going up and playing festivals in the heat of the blazing summer and going to the stage in his wheelchair. He was about the music! Most people would have stayed home, but Josh still had a lot of music to play.

I was at the IBMA Fan Fest in 2006, getting ready to go play, and Dan Hays and Carl Jackson came to me and said, "We just found out Josh Graves passed away." They asked if we would announce it on our show, and we did. The next day we got together a bunch of Dobro players and played a tribute to him. I don't think Josh was done. I hope there are still a lot of people out there that will keep playing and remembering his stuff, because he left us a lot to listen to!

Phil Leadbetter, a native of Knoxville, Tennessee, was voted Dobro Player of the Year by the International Bluegrass Music Association in 2005. He has appeared with Grandpa Jones, Vern Gosdin, J. D. Crowe, Wildfire, and Grasstowne. This tribute is based upon a 2009 interview conducted by Pat Ahrens.

➤ Marty Stuart

The first memory I have of Josh Graves is seeing him on the Flatt and Scruggs television show when I was a kid. I loved his hat, his gold tooth, and his guitar—although I didn't know what it was at the time. He looked more like the black juke joint cats I had met at the Busy Bee Café in Philadelphia, Mississippi, than the country pickers I followed.

Josh was the first country musician I ever witnessed who unapologetically played white man's blues. I loved that about him, and it touched me early on.

One of his last shows was the one he did with us, *Live at the Ryman*, in July 2003. After he passed away, I went back through his career and the early work he did with people like Mac Wiseman and Wilma Lee and Stoney Cooper. He was traditional—rooted in the Cliff Carlisle/Brother Oswald era—but he never stopped innovating. His works were instant classics at every turn.

Uncle Josh was worthy of his praise. If you subtracted his contribution from the body of country music, there would be an enormous void. Generations after generations will keep discovering Josh Graves, the way they will Johnny Cash, Bob Dylan, Bill Monroe, and Hank Williams.

He touched people in country and bluegrass, but also in folk, blues, and rock and roll. At the end of his life when I visited him, there were gold records on the wall, his IBMA Hall of Fame plaque, and a bronze bust someone had made for him.

But his biggest award was Evelyn and the home on Chadwell Drive that they made for themselves—and for every picker who needed help, love, and an open door. That stands as a legacy, beyond his playing. Josh and Evelyn touched a lot of lives.

Marty Stuart, a member of the Grand Ole Opry, *is a native of Philadelphia, Mississippi. He joined Lester Flatt and the Nashville Grass at the age of thirteen on mandolin and lead guitar and later worked with Doc Watson and Johnny Cash before forming his own act in the 1980s. A former president of the Country Music Foundation, Stuart lovingly preserves the history of country music in his photographs, writing, and collections.*

Josh, "Julie," and "Cliff" (with the Seahorse Inlay), the Two Main Instruments Played by Josh Graves between 1956 and 2006

Bobby Wolfe

Josh acquired "Julie" in late 1955 or early 1956. Negotiations were going on in December 1955, and it was in his hands prior to March 1956. This is based on letters between Josh, his wife Evelyn, and "Julie's" previous owner, Henry "Red" Harrocks, who, according to Josh, lived in Johnstown, Pennsylvania. "Julie" was used by Josh on most of his Flatt and Scruggs recordings, until their breakup in 1969.

"Julie" was a standard round-neck Model 27 California-built Dobro, serial number 7673, with a parallelogram hole sound well. It most likely was built in early 1935, possibly late 1934.

At some unknown date, Josh sold "Julie" to a friend in Texas, who kept it for about a year and then gave it back to Josh, saying that was where "Julie" should be. It was later stolen when Josh was with the Earl Scruggs Revue, playing a show date at a Loew's theater in Syracuse, New York. It was recovered from Syracuse three years later.

"Julie" was retired in March 1985, when Josh started playing "Cliff." Newly restored and refinished, "Cliff" was a standard Regal-made Model 37 with a square neck. It had no serial number. This was common for many Regal-made boxes of that era. "Cliff" was owned and played by Cliff Carlisle, who later gave it to Josh. It was the same as the two Regal-made Model 37s owned and played for many years by Mike Auldridge, except that Mike's had serial numbers 401 and 426. All three were made of birch plywood with fake mahogany grain applied.

Josh asked in 1984 if I could restore "Cliff." I looked at it and told him I could, but it would have to be completely stripped of the finish and that I would not be able to restore the fake mahogany grain. I told him I could do a sunburst finish that would be similar to other boxes of that time, but it would obviously not be a Model 37 mahogany-looking finish. That was OK with him.

Then he gave me the two pearl seahorses and said he wanted them inlaid on the upper bout. I didn't want to do that (I wanted to keep it as original as possible), but he insisted. He said some friends in Louisiana, or maybe Mississippi, had made them for him, and he wanted them on it. I reluctantly agreed.

Josh had friends all over the country he would stay with at times, sometimes between show dates, so he wouldn't have to make the long trip back to Nashville. This was the case in Louisiana. He made it a point to go there about once a year to visit and pick. I sometimes think Louisiana was one of the sources of his picking style.

"Cliff" was in bad shape—loose joints, bare wood showing all over, and with miscellaneous damage, binding loose and coming off, and so on. I stripped it, did the repairs, and after dropping the seahorses on the floor a few times (they didn't break), I inlaid them and refinished the box.

It was completed in November of 1984. I delivered it to him at a playing date (at another of those friends' houses, in Spruce Pine, North Carolina) in March of 1985. He played it, and "Julie" was retired that night. To the best of my knowledge, Josh played "Cliff" as his regular box from then until his death in 2006, except for the times he was endorsing some other instrument. The main one of these was a Gibson/Dobro, when they came out with the Uncle Josh model. I'm not sure of the others he endorsed during this period.

I have before-and-after pictures of "Cliff" and pictures of "Julie" taken the night she was retired.

APPENDIX B

Josh's Repertoire: Tunes and Songs He Featured While a Member of the Foggy Mountain Boys, 1955–1969

Stacy Phillips

This is a tentative list of all the tunes that featured Josh Graves as a member of the Foggy Mountain Boys in which he was featured on an instrumental or sang at least one solo section. I'm sure there were a few things that never got recorded. Thanks to Russ Hooper, Mike Auldridge, Bobby Wolfe, and especially Frank Godbey, for help in compiling this list.

Instrumentals

"Carroll County Blues"
"Down in the Valley"
"Fireball"
"Foggy Mountain Rock"
"I'll Be All Smiles Tonight"
"Just Joshing"
"Maiden's Prayer"
"Maggie Blues"
"Pass Me Not, O Gentle Savior"
"Rainbow"
"Rockaway"
"Steel Guitar Blues"
"Steel Guitar Chimes"
"Worried Steel Blues" (Josh's first part is almost the same as his solo on "Shuckin' the Corn")

Songs (mostly with harmony from Jake Tullock)

"Alimony Blues"
"Baby You Gotta Quit That Noise"
"Big Ball's in Brooklyn"
"Columbus Stockade Blues"
"The Crawdad Song"
"Don't Make Me Go to Bed and I'll Be Good"
"Eight More Miles to Louisville"
"Ground Hog"
"Hand Me Down My Walkin' Cane"
"I Don't Want Your Greenback Dollar"
"I'll Always Be Waiting for You"
"I'll Be Better Off without You"
"I'm Changing the Words to My Love Song of You"
"(I'm Going) Down, Down, Down"
"Lonely"
"Maybe Next Week, Some Time"
"Mountain Dew"
"New River Train"
"Nobody's Business"
"Rabbit in a Log" (also known as "Feast Here Tonight")
"Run Little Johnny"
"Sputnik Dog"
"Stuck Up Blues"
"Worried Man Blues"
"You Live in a World All Your Own"

NOTES

Foreword

1. Dobro is a registered trademark of the Gibson Guitar Corporation.

Editor's Introduction

1. Burkett Howard "Uncle Josh" Graves (1927–2006), a member of the Bluegrass Hall of Fame, was the undisputed father of the Dobro (resonator) guitar in bluegrass music.

2. The original transcripts and my edits have been placed on deposit at the International Bluegrass Music Museum in Owensboro, Kentucky.

3. The term *resophonic* refers to an acoustic string instrument whose sound is produced by one or more metal cones (resonators) instead of or in addition to a wooden soundboard.

Author's Introduction

1. The term *brogue,* which often refers to an Irish or Scottish accent, is used here by Josh to describe his southern rural expressions.

2. The number of grandchildren was twelve when Josh was interviewed. There are seventeen as of 2011.

Chapter 1. 1927–1942, A Tennessee Childhood

1. Between 1935 and 1943, the Works Progress Administration provided almost eight million jobs.

2. The Civilian Conservation Corps was a public work relief program for unemployed men, focused on natural resource conservation, from 1933 to 1942.

3. Burley is a thin-bodied, air-cured tobacco grown mainly in Kentucky.

4. Buck Jones (1891–1942, real name Charles Frederick Gebhart) was an American motion picture star of the 1920s, 1930s, and 1940s, known for his many popular Western movies.

5. On a mid-1950s Flatt and Scruggs radio show, Lester Flatt referred to Josh as "The Maryville Flash." Ironically, Maryville College is now the headquarters each June for Steve Kaufman's Acoustic Kamps, including a Dobro workshop.

6. The nut is a thin strip of wood, bone, plastic, or metal, with notches that guide the strings from a string instrument's peghead to the fingerboard. Raising the nut of a standard guitar allows it to be fretted Hawaiian style, with a metal bar held above the open strings.

7. "Jumping" Bill Carlisle (1908–2003) appeared on the *Grand Ole Opry* until his death at the age of ninety-four.

8. The Delco-Light was a small internal combustion generator with battery, intended to provide a source of electric illumination and mechanical power to rural residents who were not yet connected to the electrical grid.

9. Beecher Kirby (1911–2002), whose stage name was Bashful Brother Oswald, replaced Clell Summey in Roy Acuff's band in 1939.

10. Roy Acuff (1903–1992) recorded "Stuck Up Blues" in April 1941.

11. George E. "Speedy" Krise (1922–2011) also wrote a number of songs recorded by Carl Butler, Little Jimmy Dickens, Mac Wiseman, and others.

12. Josh turned fourteen in 1942.

13. North Carolinians Walter (1910–1971) and Homer "Bill" (1912–2002) Callahan were a popular mandolin-guitar duet of the 1930s and early 1940s. Several of their songs, notably "They're at Rest Together" and "Sweet Thing," have been covered by bluegrass artists.

14. The trade name Graphophone was used into the 1920s or 1930s by Columbia Records as the name for their version of the phonograph.

15. The word *harp* is used here to refer to a harmonica, also known as a mouth harp.

Chapter 2. 1942–1955, A Musical Apprenticeship

1. Window cards, 14 × 22–inch pasteboard advertisements, were placed in store and theater windows to promote upcoming live performances and movie showings.

2. Esco Hankins (1924–1990) was a regional country singer and recording artist in the Roy Acuff mold.

3. Cas Walker (1902–1998) was a successful grocery entrepreneur and politician who sponsored long-running Knoxville country radio and television programs. The Everly Brothers and Dolly Parton got their start on the *Cas Walker Show.*

4. Wade Mainer (1907–2011) was still performing until just before his death at the age of 104.

5. Cal Stewart (1856–1919), from Charlotte County, Virginia, was a pioneer in vaudeville and early sound recordings. He is best remembered for comic monologues in which he played "Uncle Josh" Weathersby, a resident of a mythical New England farming town called Punkin Center. "Uncle Josh on a Bicycle" is one of Cal Stewart's well-known monologues. Earl Bolick (1919–1998) of the Blue Sky Boys also played an "Uncle Josh" character on southern radio broadcasts in the 1940s and possibly earlier.

6. "My Dixie Home" was recorded in a slow tempo by Asa Jenkins and Carson Robison (1928), Loy Bodine and Howard Keesee (1931), Asa Martin and James Roberts (1933), and the Monroe Brothers (in 1936 as "I'm Thinking Tonight of the Old Folks"). Bill Monroe never recorded it commercially with the Blue Grass Boys, but a blindingly fast version, featuring Scruggs's banjo, survives on a bootleg album of their 1946–1948 radio broadcasts.

7. "Uncle Dave" Macon (1870–1952) was a banjo-playing singer/comedian who became the first featured star of the *Grand Ole Opry* in 1925. The story Josh recalls occurred in 1945, as Macon's prominence was being usurped by Roy Acuff, Bill Monroe, and Ernest Tubb.

8. Sparta, Tennessee, was Lester Flatt's hometown.

9. During Josh's second stint with Esco Hankins, the band worked out of Lexington, Kentucky. Lester Flatt, Earl Scruggs, and the Foggy Mountain Boys were also based there, from the fall of 1949 to the spring of 1950 and again from the fall of 1950 to September, 1951.

10. He refers to Beecher "Bashful Brother Oswald" Kirby, the most prominent Dobro player of the time, who was appearing and recording with Roy Acuff and the Smoky Mountain Boys.

11. This was during Josh's second stint with Esco Hankins, when that band and Flatt and Scruggs both spent time in Lexington, Kentucky.

12. This is a reference to cam tuners, which Earl Scruggs used to switch from G to D tuning in the middle of such tunes as "Earl's Breakdown."

13. WWVA-AM's clear-channel 50,000–watt signal can be heard at night throughout the eastern United States and most of Canada.

14. Walt Saunders, who writes the column "Notes and Queries" for *Bluegrass Unlimited* magazine, stated in a 2010 personal communication, "Buck worked with Charlie Bailey in 1954, between the tour with Wilma Lee and Stoney, and probably Toby Stroud. Anyway, I know that Charlie picked him up when he left the Coopers, which would have probably been in early 1954. They worked at WWVA in Wheeling for maybe three months."

1. This is a reference to an African American folktale, adapted by Joel Chandler Harris in *Uncle Remus* (1881). Br'er Rabbit employs reverse psychology by begging his captor, the Fox, to do anything but throw him into the briar patch.

2. Columbia 21051, recorded on September 2, 1955, and released on February 20, 1956.

3. Presumably they heard the song on the radio or a jukebox audible from the bus (Josh doesn't explain).

4. Dobro players Russ Hooper, Mike Auldridge, and Stacy Phillips are all certain that Josh's Dobro work on "Blue Ridge Cabin Home" (September 2, 1955) was played in the key of A with a capo. All three remember Josh saying that, for the session, he adapted a metal can/bottle opener (familiarly known at the time as a "church key") as a makeshift capo. Perhaps Graves's memory has combined two different ad hoc capos. Stacy remembers reading that Lester Flatt asked him not to use a capo anymore; personal communications, 2009.

5. Earl and Louise Scruggs had an auto accident in October 1955 while on their way to North Carolina to visit his seriously ill mother. Earl was in the hospital for several weeks and off the road for months.

6. According to the *Encyclopedia of Country Music* (New York: Oxford University Press, 2004), Cohen E. Williams and his sons, Cohen T. Williams and Joe Williams, bought Nashville's Royal, Barry-Carter Mills in 1941, renaming it Martha White Foods.

7. Recorded in December 1962; released in August 1963. Even in New York City, members of the audience could be heard requesting the Martha White theme song, to Lester Flatt's audible surprise.

8. A number of the early Flatt and Scruggs television shows have recently been found and released in DVD format on the Shanachie label in cooperation with the Country Music Hall of Fame. On these programs, Josh's roles included the reading of mailed-in requests for dedications.

9. Hadacol was a vitamin supplement that contained 12 percent alcohol. Until the company's collapse in 1951, it sponsored Hadacol Caravans that attracted huge crowds with Hollywood film stars, country, jazz, and blues artists.

10. He refers to the Dobro guitar previously owned by Cliff Carlisle.

11. The Timberliners.

12. Meaning that the entire band played over a single, omnidirectional microphone. Curly Seckler was quoted as saying, "Flatt before he died, he said 'All them cords is good for is someone to fall down and break their neck.' He never did go modern much"; from Barry Willis, *America's Music: Bluegrass* (Franktown, Colo.: Pine Valley Music, 1998), 147.

13. Carl Smith (1927–2010) was a commercial country star from the 1950s to the 1970s.

14. The Foggy Mountain Boys' famous stage choreography can be seen in DVD releases of the Flatt and Scruggs TV show.

15. Paul Warren (1918–1978) was the Foggy Mountain Boys' fiddler from 1954 to 1969. He stayed with Lester Flatt as a member of the Nashville Grass until 1977.

Chapter 4. 1955–1969, Part 2, Life on the Road and the Breakup

1. The reference to "signing the paper" wasn't explained.

2. This is a reference to the Ryman Auditorium in downtown Nashville, home of the *Grand Ole Opry* from 1943 to 1974.

3. Jimmy Martin, leader of the Sunny Mountain Boys, died in 2005.

4. Benny Martin (1928–2001) was a country and bluegrass fiddler and singer. A solo artist by the mid-1950s, Martin had earlier been in bands with Bill Monroe, Roy Acuff, Flatt and Scruggs, and Johnnie and Jack.

5. *The Beverly Hillbillies* was a popular CBS television sitcom that aired from 1962 to 1971. Flatt and Scruggs performed the instrumental backing for the theme song and appeared in several episodes.

6. He probably refers to the band's young, nonrural audience at the time.

7. Hugely successful for two decades on the air, on records, and on stage, Flatt and Scruggs finally split after differences about musical direction. Earl Scruggs wanted to play more modern music with his sons. Uncomfortable singing Bob Dylan and other folk material demanded by a Columbia record contract, Lester Flatt headed off on his own to play a more traditional brand of bluegrass. Their final joint appearance on the *Grand Ole Opry* was on February 22, 1969. After it was discovered that the duo's contract required one more Columbia album, they recorded *Final Fling*. Those sessions ended on August 22, 1969, the last time Lester Flatt and Earl Scruggs played together. According to an interview with Earl Scruggs on Doug Hutchens's radio show, *Bluegrass Today*, quoted by Barry Willis in *America's Music: Bluegrass* (1989), Earl visited Lester in the hospital shortly before Flatt's death in May 1979 and reported that the two discussed plans for reunion concerts that never materialized.

8. Lance LeRoy worked with Lester Flatt before the breakup as an accountant and later became manager and booking agent for Lester Flatt and the Nashville Grass.

Chapter 5. 1969–1994, King of the Dobro

1. Apparently Vic Jordan returned to the band after being fired.

2. Bill Monroe produced a famous bluegrass festival at his Brown County Jamboree Park in the southern Indiana village of Bean Blossom.

3. This was the end of a feud going back to 1955, when Flatt and Scruggs were invited to join the *Grand Ole Opry* over Bill Monroe's objections.

4. According to Stacy Phillips, who was present, "For Dobro players, one of the highlights of that set was Josh's very upfront fills when Bill Monroe sang lead. Given Monroe's cryptic, but seemingly negative, comments about the Dobro in bluegrass, it was obvious that Josh was laying the accompaniment on thick for Bill"; personal communication, 2009.

5. Charlie McCoy's instrumental version of Merle Haggard and Buck Owens's "Today I Started Loving You Again" was McCoy's highest and first charting single, reaching number 16 on the Billboard country charts in 1972.

6. He refers to Jake Tullock.

7. Now Nashville International Airport.

8. Around Thanksgiving 1975.

9. This interview was conducted in 1994.

10. Kenny Baker (1926–2011) played fiddle with Bill Monroe and the Blue Grass Boys for almost twenty years, in four different hitches, beginning in 1957. The last ended on October 12, 1984.

11. *Something Different,* Puritan 5001, 1972; *Bucktime,* Puritan 5005, 1974, since reissued on CD as *The Puritan Sessions,* Rebel CD-1108. On these projects, Josh played Dobro and sang. Kenny Baker played finger-style guitar.

12. The National Council for the Arts' "Masters of the Folk Violin" toured the nation four times between 1988 and 1995. Other performers included Michael Doucet, Claude Williams, Joe Cormier, Seamus Connolly, Brendan Mulvihill, Natalie McMaster, and Howard Armstrong.

13. Because Josh's primary instrument didn't require the fingers of his left hand to touch the strings, he had not developed the tough calluses that other string musicians must have to play comfortably.

Chapter 6. A Man of Many Talents

1. Wilma Lee and Stoney Cooper's single of "Come Walk with Me" on Hickory Records was on the Billboard country charts for twenty-six weeks in 1959, peaking at number 4.

2. As early as the 1920s, country musicians found that publishing royalties could exceed their share of royalties for record sales. Buying and selling of composer credits was a common practice.

3. Roy Madison "Junior" Huskey Jr. (1928–1971) was a well-known Nashvill studio bass player, not to be confused with his son Roy Milton Huskey (195/ 1997), also an in-demand session bass player.

4. "If You're Ever Going to Love Me" was first recorded by the Kentucky Colonels in 1963 on the album *Bluegrass America* (Briar M109). Stacy Phillips says, "Dobro player Leroy Mack capoed up nine frets on that one."

5. "Fireball," from the album *World's Greatest Show* (Sugar Hill Records), was named Best Country Instrumental Performance in the 1983 Grammy awards.

6. R. Q. Jones.

7. He refers to a cross-hatched design.

8. *Sing Away the Pain* (CMH Records, 1979).

9. *Just Joshin'* by Uncle Josh (Graves) and Cousin Jake (Tullock) may have been the first bluegrass "solo project"—an album released by musicians away from their regular touring band, often involving members of several different groups. Cowboy Carl reissued it on vinyl in 1979, and Red Clay Records reissued it on CD in 2005.

10. According to Stacy Phillips, "Josh played guitar and sang on about half the cuts. In fact, on the track of 'Oswald's Chimes,' Brother Oswald played Dobro."

11. The year was 1975.

12. He refers to tips, placed in a jar or basket, rather than a contracted fee or "the door" (the entire gate receipts when a bar or restaurant makes its money on the food and drink).

13. At the time of the interview, Owensboro, Kentucky, was the site of the annual convention and trade show of the International Bluegrass Music Association.

14. A reference to Josh's wife Evelyn.

Chapter 7. Reflections on Bluegrass Old and New

1. This is a reference to the Monroe Brothers, who recorded between 1936 and 1938, before Bill struck out on his own and founded the Blue Grass Boys.

2. Josh's disparaging references to Bill Monroe's timing with the Monroe Brothers may be a bit unfair. Their acceleration could have been a conscious effect to build excitement. It is also possible that Bill was following his older brother's looser sense of timing. Charlie's later recordings demonstrate ragged rhythms; Bill's pre-Scruggs records with the Blue Grass Boys are more syncopated than anything the Monroe Brothers did, but regular in meter.

3. *Charlie Monroe on the Noonday Jamboree* (County 538, 1974).

4. According to Stacy Phillips, "The Bill Monroe quote about Dobro that I remember was from a radio interview. When asked why he didn't have a Dobro in his group, Monroe said, 'I wouldn't have one.' Interestingly, Bill Monroe and Josh

Graves both played on Bill's 'The Old Kentucky Blues,' on Gary Brewer's album *Guitar,* Copper Creek Records, 1995."

5. According to Dobro expert Bobby Wolfe, "In the mid-'60s there was a club on Nashville's Printers Alley called The Black Poodle. Bill Monroe was appearing there one night during the DJ Convention in October. This would have been around the time Richard Greene was fiddling, Lamar Grier was on banjo and Peter Rowan was on guitar. Bill had Tut Taylor and a young Curtis Burch on stage for a couple of numbers. That was not one but two Dobros on stage with Bill Monroe! I was there"; personal communication, 2009.

6. Interviewer Barry Willis was a commercial pilot at the time.

7. The Sauceman Brothers were contemporaries with Flatt and Scruggs and the Stanley Brothers in the early bluegrass scene.

8. Billy Grammer had a top-ten country hit with "Gotta Travel On" in 1959.

9. The Dobro is tuned to a major chord and played with a bar.

10. John Hartford's 1967 recording of "(Good Old Electric) Washing Machine (Circa 1943)" includes a humorous verbal interpretation of an old-fashioned washing machine.

11. Here Josh is referring to the death of Earl and Louise Scruggs's youngest son, Steve, on September 23, 1992. Louise Scruggs died on February 2, 2006, after extended respiratory problems.

12. The Bluegrass Trust Fund, administered by the International Bluegrass Music Association, was established in 1987 as a means to offer financial assistance to bluegrass music professionals in time of emergency need.

13. The International Bluegrass Music Association's trade show was held in Owensboro, Kentucky, from 1986 to 1996; in Louisville, Kentucky, from 1997 to 2004; and in Nashville, Tennessee, since then.

Chapter 8. A Family Musical Legacy

1. This is a reference to Josh's wife, Evelyn.

2. Josh Graves lived to the age of seventy-nine, performing almost to the end despite serious health problems. He died on September 30, 2006, while the International Bluegrass Music Association World of Bluegrass was going on in Nashville. Josh had planned a special "Legends" appearance that evening with former Foggy Mountain Boys Mac Wiseman, Curly Seckler, and Everett Lilly. At that concert, in his memory, eight bluegrass Dobro players performed his instrumental showpieces "Fireball" and "Flatt Lonesome."

Chapter 9. Testimony from Josh Graves's Contemporaries and Those He Influenced

1. This is a reference to Dobro artist Bashful Brother Oswald (1911–2002), a longtime member of Roy Acuff's Smoky Mountain Boys.

2. The International Bluegrass Music Association.

3. Society for the Preservation of Bluegrass Music of America's annual Awards Show and Convention, held in Nashville, Tennessee.

4. This is a reference to the TV comedy *Sanford and Son,* from the 1970s, in which Redd Foxx's character would seek sympathy by feigning a heart attack and calling upon his late wife, Elizabeth.

INDEX

reconciliation with Bill Monroe, 47; shuns Josh Graves, 55–56

Flatt and Scruggs and the Foggy Mountain Boys, vii, 22–33, 34–44, 70–72, 79, 92, 93, 98; band bus, 26, 35–35, 38; band name, 44; breakup, 42–44; finances, 24, 36–37, 43; formation, 70–71; influence on others, 76, 97; play college campuses, 29, 34, 42; road life, 35; television, 26, 43, 111

Flatt and Scruggs at Carnegie Hall! (sound recording), 26, 32

"Flatt Lonesome," 96, 110

"Flint Hill Special," 19, 31

Florence, Ala., 26

Foggy Mountain Banjo (sound recording), 105

"Foggy Mountain Breakdown," 49, 71

"Foggy Mountain Rock," 96, 98, 99

"Foggy Mountain Special," 100

"Fox Chase," 9

Franklin, N.C., 35

Gadsden, Ala., 26

Gatlinburg, Tenn., 13

Georgia, 35

"Getaway," 100

Gettysburg, Pa., 21

Goldsmith, Thomas, xi

"Good Things Outweigh the Bad," 96

gospel songs, 67

"Gotta Travel On," 72

Grammer, Billy, 72

Grammy Award, 60

Grand Ole Opry, 15–16, 25, 39

Graphophone, 9

Grass Valley, Calif., 56

Grass Valley Bluegrass Festival (Grass Valley, Calif.), 103

Grateful Dead, 49

Graves, "Billy" Troy. *See* Graves, William "Billy" Troy (son)

Graves, Bryan (son), 15, 79–81

Graves, Buck. *See* Graves, Burkett Howard "Uncle Josh"

Graves, Buddy Wayne (brother), 2

Graves, Burkett Howard "Uncle Josh": alcohol, 12, 50, 51, 59, 66–68; and Kenny Baker, 53–56, 77; birth, vii, 1–2; Cherokee blood, 2, 15, 84; children, 79–80; comedian, vii, 14–15, 22, 27–28, 56, 93; death, viii; drugs, 67–68; as emcee, 56; family, 2, 9; fishing, 86; heart problems, 57; influence on others, 76–77, 94, 96, 98–115; influences, blues, viii, 1, 5–6, 30–31, 58, 66–67, 107, 111; influences, bottleneck, 5; influences, musical, 4–9, 12; leaves the Earl Scruggs Revue, 50; leaves Flatt and Scruggs, 40; leaves the Nashville Grass, 46; leg amputations, 105, 108, 110; management skills, 46; marriage, 15; nickname, 3, 14–15, 20, 90; occupations, 10; on fiddle, 14; on guitar, 5, 14, 32–33, 42; on mandolin, 14, 90, 91; on string bass, vii, 13, 14, 23, 56; pay, 13, 18, 36–37, 40, 45, 46, 49, 65; picking style, vii, 12, 18, 19, 32–33, 69, 87, 90, 93, 96; recording sessions, 64; schooling, 10; songwriting, 58–60, 95–96

Graves, Burkett "Josh Jr." (son), 15, 79–80

Graves, Evelyn Hurst (wife), xi, 15, 37, 49, 55, 59–60, 79, 87, 89, 91, 93

Graves, Geneva (sister), 2

Graves, Harlan Richard "Dick" (brother), 2, 85

Graves, Harold Ray (brother), 2

Graves, Jake "Uncle Jake," 83

Graves, Jewel (sister), 2

Graves, "Josh." *See* Graves, Burkett Howard "Uncle Josh"

Graves, Linda (daughter), 15, 79

Graves, Sara Elizabeth. *See* Thomas, Sara Elizabeth (mother)

Graves, Tim (nephew), 82, 103, 109, 110

Graves, Troy (father), 2, 4–6, 10; drinking, 5

Graves, "Uncle Josh." *See* Graves, Burkett Howard "Uncle Josh"

Graves, William "Billy" Troy (son), 15, 65–66, 79, 80, 86

The Graves Digger (sound recording), 101

Great Dobro Sessions (sound recording), 99, 106

"Great Speckled Bird," 66

Fred Bartenstein has performed many roles in bluegrass music, including magazine editor, broadcaster, musician, festival MC, talent director, scholar, and consultant. He lives in Yellow Springs, Ohio.

Neil Rosenberg is Professor Emeritus of Folklore at Memorial University (St. John's, Newfoundland and Labrador, Canada). He is a leading scholar of bluegrass music, author of *Bluegrass: A History* (1985, 2005), coauthor of *The Music of Bill Monroe* (2007) and *Bluegrass Odyssey* (2001), and author of numerous articles and liner notes.

America's Music: From the Pilgrims to the Present (rev. 3d ed.) *Gilbert Chase*

Secular Music in Colonial Annapolis: The Tuesday Club, 1745–56 *John Barry Talley*

Bibliographical Handbook of American Music *D. W. Krummel*

Goin' to Kansas City *Nathan W. Pearson, Jr.*

"Susanna," "Jeanie," and "The Old Folks at Home": The Songs of Stephen C. Foster
 from His Time to Ours (2d ed.) *William W. Austin*

Songprints: The Musical Experience of Five Shoshone Women *Judith Vander*

"Happy in the Service of the Lord": Afro-American Gospel Quartets in
 Memphis *Kip Lornell*

Paul Hindemith in the United States *Luther Noss*

"My Song Is My Weapon": People's Songs, American Communism, and the Politics of
 Culture, 1930–50 *Robbie Lieberman*

Chosen Voices: The Story of the American Cantorate *Mark Slobin*

Theodore Thomas: America's Conductor and Builder of Orchestras, 1835–1905
 Ezra Schabas

"The Whorehouse Bells Were Ringing" and Other Songs Cowboys Sing *Collected and
 Edited by Guy Logsdon*

Crazeology: The Autobiography of a Chicago Jazzman *Bud Freeman, as Told to
 Robert Wolf*

Discoursing Sweet Music: Brass Bands and Community Life in Turn-of-the-Century
 Pennsylvania *Kenneth Kreitner*

Mormonism and Music: A History *Michael Hicks*

Voices of the Jazz Age: Profiles of Eight Vintage Jazzmen *Chip Deffaa*

Pickin' on Peachtree: A History of Country Music in Atlanta, Georgia
 Wayne W. Daniel

Bitter Music: Collected Journals, Essays, Introductions, and Librettos *Harry Partch;
 edited by Thomas McGeary*

Ethnic Music on Records: A Discography of Ethnic Recordings Produced in the
 United States, 1893 to 1942 *Richard K. Spottswood*

Downhome Blues Lyrics: An Anthology from the Post–World War II Era
 Jeff Todd Titon

Ellington: The Early Years *Mark Tucker*

Chicago Soul *Robert Pruter*

That Half-Barbaric Twang: The Banjo in American Popular Culture *Karen Linn*

Hot Man: The Life of Art Hodes *Art Hodes and Chadwick Hansen*

The Erotic Muse: American Bawdy Songs (2d ed.) *Ed Cray*

Barrio Rhythm: Mexican American Music in Los Angeles *Steven Loza*

The Creation of Jazz: Music, Race, and Culture in Urban America *Burton W. Peretti*

Charles Martin Loeffler: A Life Apart in Music *Ellen Knight*

Club Date Musicians: Playing the New York Party Circuit *Bruce A. MacLeod*

The University of Illinois Press
is a founding member of the
Association of American University Presses.

Designed by Erin Kirk New
Composed in 10.4/14.5 Adobe Chapparal
with Ironmonger display
by Erin Kirk New
for the University of Illinois Press
Manufactured by Sheridan Books, Inc.

University of Illinois Press
1325 South Oak Street
Champaign, IL 61820–6903
www.press.uillinois.edu